Affiliation	*Affirmation*	*Achievement*
Forming Bonds G3	**Confirming Wholeness** G4	**Ensuring Growth** G5
Matching **Sharing** R3	*Ministry* **Serving** R4	*Mastery* **Skills** R5
Theory *Z* **Consensus** I3	Theory *M* **Confusion** I4	Theory *I* **Competency** I5
Information **Facts and Beliefs** D3	*Imagination* **Hopes and Dreams** D	*...ality* **...elf- Determination** D5
Elements **Theory – Where Success Is Born** S3	*Exercises* **Activities – Where Success Is Nurtured** S4	*Experiments* **To-Do's – Where Success Happens** S5

The Table of Success Elements

THEORY *I*

THE METHODOLOGY FOR SUCCESS

Clifford I. Sears

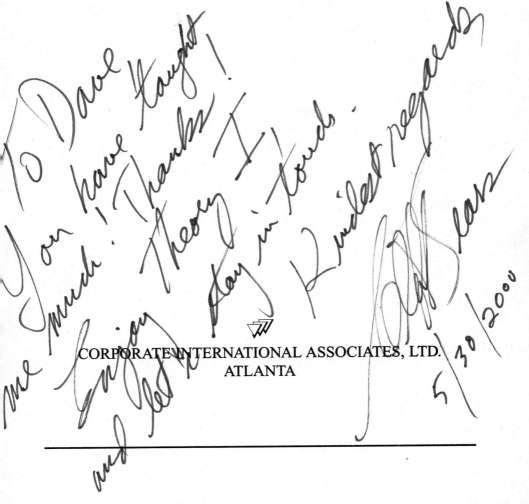

CORPORATE INTERNATIONAL ASSOCIATES, LTD.
ATLANTA

First Edition, September 1997

Jacket and book design by Robert Aulicino, Pro-Art Graphic Design
Printing and book binding by Banta Book Group, Banta Corporation
Printed in the United States of America

Publisher's Cataloging-in-Publication
(Provided by Quality Books, Inc.)

Sears, Clifford I.
  Theory I : the methodology for success / Clifford I. Sears. —
  1st ed.
  p. cm.
  Registered trademark symbol follows italic Roman capital letter
I on t.p.
  Includes index.
  Preassigned LCCN: 97-66729
  ISBN: 0-9634993-1-9

  1. Success—Psychological aspects.   2. Self-actualization
(Psychology)   I. Title.

BF637.S8S43 1997   158
                                    QBI97-40463

Dedicated to my wife,
Carol,
with all my love,
all my life

CONTENTS IN BRIEF

Contents

ACKNOWLEDGMENTS

As I complete the long journey for writing this book, I want to express thanks for support and good wishes from those around me for whom I have the highest regard and gratitude.

First of all, I would like to thank Carol, my wife of over 30 years, who had honest and very reasonable doubts from time to time, but who tirelessly stood by me when my dreams appeared impossible; and my children, Craig and Cheri, through whom I have vicariously lived a second childhood, since in my own I was never an honor student, an accomplished musician, or an All-American swimmer or diver.

I am exceptionally grateful to my longest-time colleague, critic, and confidant, who has been by my side for countless hours discussing the content, context, and structure of my work. His role was unique in devotion and expertise that increased year after year. His work has been essential in the translation of my discussions and seminars into print, leaving no hole unfilled. He is my son, Craig. My daughter, Cheri, became a critical factor in completing my work by inspiring me with her courage in achieving things most people considered impossible. Her confidence and perseverance led me to new heights in understanding. She never doubted my success for a moment. For that and for everything else, I am most thankful.

The love of my late parents, John and Helen Sears, guided me through my formative years and gave me the freedom to develop into a person who I hope lives up to their memory. The support of my five older siblings, Lois Ann, Joan, Kay, Jennylou, and John, fostered my interest in promoting personal understanding and happiness.

For his staunch efforts in adjusting, arranging, and preparing the manuscript for publication, I would like to thank my superb editor, Richard Weaver. Let's do it again.

Space precludes the inclusion of a complete list of all who have offered personal encouragement during the evolution of my ideas: Terry Jenkins (Executive Producer of an award-winning film on this subject), Lew Gray (former Division President and Corporate Vice President of IBM), Lloyd Dobyns (for his strong belief and support for my work), Ila Sanders (curriculum manager for the first courses on this subject), Jim Lemser (course manager for these early programs), Ann Johnson (art director for program presentations), J. Melvin England (for his diligent efforts in protecting the copyright of this manuscript), Richard J. Meinhold (for his detailed scrutiny and comments on the manuscript), Tom Murphy and Melissa Thibodeau (printing consultants), and my esteemed associates, Jason Vaniman, Gerry Cohen, and Dr. Lane Alderman. A special thanks is also due to my students, colleagues, managers, and customers whom I have had the distinct privilege of working with during my twenty years in the computer industry. And, of course, the many people who expressed their thoughts following seminars and who showed tremendous belief and interest in my work, I thank you as well. I only hope Theory *I* will speed the fulfillment of all your dreams. You deserve it.

Lastly, the works of my distant relative, Mark Twain (Samuel Clemens), showed me the enduring power of the written word. Perhaps it was a little spark of him that made me curious enough to seek out new, uncharted waters.

INTRODUCTION

Theory $I_®$ - THE METHODOLOGY FOR SUCCESS

Many people searching for the path to success have become frustrated by outdated business models, complex analyses, and platitudes on the promises of tomorrow. In this book we will learn how consistent success can be reached with the implementation of the Theory I methodology. Its use begins a process of change on an institutional level that begins with one individual at a time. Success is the fulfillment of goals by all parties involved. Theory I enables people to satisfy personal interests in conjunction with meeting corporate objectives.

This balance of personal and corporate interests begins when a system is put in place to allow each individual to have a vested interest in the company and vice versa. The system is a support structure for success, and it is built on levels of persistence in motivation, conscientiousness in development, and accountability in performance.

Rapidly changing work environments demand precise, rapid-fire responses that target barriers and satisfy needs. The value of talent and knowledge is in their application, and Theory I is uniquely structured to harness them. The synergy of talents and ideas and the atmosphere that fosters that synergy is possible only through using the Theory I methodology.

Theory I provides us with the tools and ability to break down all problems into elements and restructure those elements through principles that become the foundation of our personalized versions of the Theory I methodology for success. After the principles are formed, strategies are then devised to apply these principles and elements within a course of action that generates the most positive results possible.

Theory *I* strategies chart out the shortest distance to meet a goal, with the least amount of effort. A multi-dimensional approach to strategy formation begins with a table that displays every element behind every decision we need to make to stay on course. The elements are organized in proper relationship to each other in this table. They have properties we can use for thorough coverage, analysis, and pathfinding that ensure success. Nothing escapes the scrutiny of this comprehensive methodology. Accurate decision making avoids irrelevant data just as a radar guided missile avoids chaff and hones in on its target; distractions are eliminated. This capability is a necessity with the abundance of choices in all of our endeavors. Theory *I* focuses us on what is necessary for success.

When we chart a course, we have to consider different directions and make a decision. Everything we learn about Theory *I* will lead us to binary decisions ("yes" or "no") about success. The subject of success is surrounded by myths and folklore that create gray areas. Lost in this confusion, we are hesitant to make any decision; often we are not even aware that alternatives exist. Through Theory *I* we can realize our potential by fully understanding what is within our reach.

Throughout this book we will define, explain, and exercise the Theory *I* methodology to create comprehensive pictures of success, and to personalize our roles in making success happen. The structure of Theory *I* is a compass that becomes easier to read with experience. In answering comprehensive questions, Theory *I* users will experience personal control, peace of mind, steady progress, and, ultimately, success. After learning Theory *I*, avoiding stress, working effectively with people, and producing success will come naturally.

ILLUSTRATIONS

CHAPTER 1

THE NEED FOR A METHODOLOGY

We begin to learn the value and scope of this subject by examining three important considerations: **Where We Find Ourselves Today, The Foundation for Success,** and **Questions that Lead Us to Success.** Next, we learn an approach for **Diagnosing Problems on the Road to Success.** We will introduce **The Critical Need for a Methodology** by defining it, reviewing a brief history, and providing examples of situations requiring methodologies (rather than application of dogma). After **Contrasting Dogma to a Methodology,** we describe the advantages of **Motivation Versus Manipulation,** as well as address opportunities and challenges. Lastly we will learn about **Elements as the Building Blocks to Success.**

Where We Find Ourselves Today

What do we expect to do this week? What are our long term expectations? What expectations do others have for us? Often, these expectations come from our bosses, clients, family, clergy, and professors. Expectations, our own and those of others, can only be met through the realization of specific challenges that we must face.

How do our performances compare to these expectations? In most cases, we probably meet the expectations so that we receive the desired reward: money, prestige, attention; it could be anything.

How often do we perform only at the expected level, when we know we are capable of more? Probably more than we are willing to admit. Why do we usually stop at expectations?

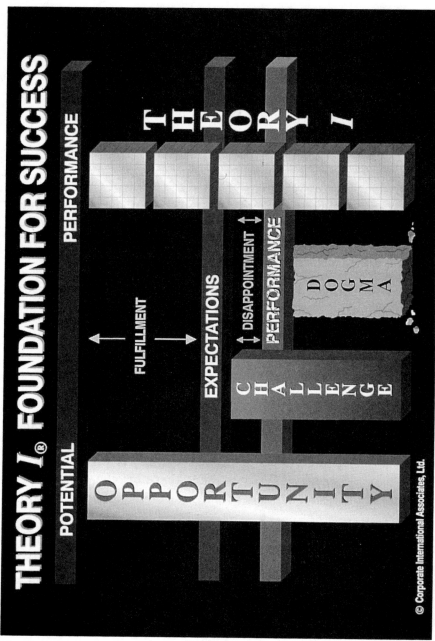

Figure 1

If we knew precisely how to gain greater reward from every opportunity in our environment, we would naturally muster the necessary effort to exceed expectations. When we exceed expectations through our performance, we receive fulfillment.

However, we do not always reach those expectations. Perhaps we are apathetic (because the barriers appear too big, or the rewards for our efforts are too little or meaningless to us). Sometimes we don't know how to meet expectations placed on us, and we become frustrated. When our performance does not meet expectations, we feel disappointment. The lower the performance and the higher the expectation, the greater the disappointment. When expectations are exceeded, to that degree we are fulfilled. Fulfillment reflects our progress in realizing our hopes, dreams, and promises, and provides us with more productive and happy business and personal lives.

We should not allow expectations to dominate our approach to completing a task; we need to focus on what will take us beyond expectations to reach our potential.

The Foundation for Success

We can reach our potential by exploring the opportunities in our environment (Figure 1). Reaching our potential requires understanding all of the components of success. Opportunity is virtually limitless. We need to know how to select and evaluate opportunities to decide which opportunities will lead us to success in meeting expectations. These chosen opportunities become our challenges. Exceeding these challenges with Theory *I* allows us to fulfill our potential.

There are two basic paths to follow for exploiting opportunities. We could choose to follow dogma. Dogma dictates a fixed general solution or frame of mind for a particular situation and has value only when future situations are identical in level and particularity of detail. We learn dogma through practices passed down through families and through businesses. Following dogma inevitably leads users to a glass barrier, where they can see success, but they are restrained from using all of their skills to obtain that success.

Circumstances are modifying or influencing factors, such as differing personalities. Situations are locations or positions with reference to environment, such as restructuring of an organization. When we combine varying circumstances within changing situations, a methodology is necessary. Learning dogma is like memorizing answers in the back of a mathematics book to the exercises at the end of each chapter. As long as our future experiences remain exactly the same as the example problems, we will meet expectations. In a changing world, the chances of producing success using dogma diminish daily. Learning a methodology teaches us the elements, principles, and strategies to solve any opportunity or challenge related to our motivation, development, or performance.

To successfully meet any challenge, we need a methodology. A true methodology is flexible so that solutions are specific to the situation. The more opportunities we are able to fully explore, the closer we come to reaching our potential. As we become more familiar with the methodology, we raise both our performance and expectations to equal our potential.

In the Foundation for Success diagram, the column on the far right represents the Theory *I* methodology. The pillar starts at the base of an opportunity and progresses beyond expectations to the full realization of potential. This pillar becomes a detailed guide to reaching this potential.

Questions that Lead Us to Success

Success is the fulfillment of potential. The extent of our success is measured in relation to our highest level of opportunities. Building the base of this new column of success begins with answers to the following questions:

> Which results assure success?
>
> How do people influence each other?
>
> When are people most effective?
>
> What affects human behavior?
>
> Where does success begin?

Answering these questions begins a process in which elements are compounded into solutions. When facing today's complex challenges and opportunities, simple success tips (dogma) collapse into useless pieces of information.

Today's more discerning success seeker wants a solid, dependable process for building success. People and corporations are ready to go beyond motivational fads, to a foundation of success knowledge that grows in significance. We need a comprehensive methodology that leads us to the complete answer. The complete answer results in personal and corporate success beyond expectations, all the way up to our fullest potential.

Over the years we have learned about people and success in bits and pieces. To become successful we must bring this knowledge together into a compatible structure where all of the pieces fit and support each other. Our formal schooling taught us about people through biology, psychology, sociology, religion, art, sports, etc. We learned about business through accounting, marketing, finance, statistics, economics, management, etc. We learned about our world and universe through chemistry, physics, geology, astronomy, etc. Each area of study adds some value to our complete pie of human understanding; however, only when we see how the pieces fit and interact do we achieve a holistic perspective. How each subject supports the others is as important as how it supports itself.

To ensure our success we need specificity in our directions and decisions. In practical application, if we were lost and needed directions, being told to, "Go about a mile north and make a right turn; proceed for about two or three miles and go left," may leave us out in the wilderness. There are so many choices along the way that general advice simply causes more frustration. We need to go beyond general words and concepts.

Diagnosing Problems on the Road to Success

Managers hire and fire people over "attitude." Attitude is a disposition where opportunities and challenges will be either seized or ignored. All too easily attitude becomes a mind-set and general description regarding another person or people. Couples get married or divorced over "attitude." Once this word is connected to "good" or "bad," people can justify any decision they make related to another human being. Do people really understand "attitude," or are they simply trying to firm up what they want to do based upon their own feelings and thinking? The following graphic (Figure 2) depicts the division of attitude into pieces (elements).

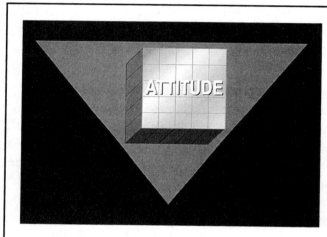

Figure 2

The Anatomy of an Attitude
We must break attitudes down into pieces to understand what brought them about.

To make decisions we need facts, not just feelings about people and situations. We need to break down facts into elements. Elements are the components of the outcome of a situation. When we have good or bad feelings, we need to identify the elements behind them. We need to understand all of the components that make up attitude.

Attitudes are very enduring. Without the proper tools (instruments that define and use elements), understanding (principles based upon relationships of elements), and sense of personal freedom (strategies to ensure personal success), attitudes can be difficult to alter in favor of the person or those around them. Since attitude is a reflection of a person's unique thinking and feelings, the path to a favorable impact must begin within the person themselves, not merely through encouraged behavioral change.

Attitudes have been approached using numerous methods of influence. *Behaviorism* is the doctrine that regards objective and accessible facts of behavior as the only proper subject for psychological study. Behaviorism depends more on stimulus-response relationships and less on individual thought processes and personality development. The term "Pavlovian dogs" can be traced to study of these reactions: Russian physiologist Ivan P. Pavlov experimented with using bells to generate salivation responses in dogs.

Attitude is the result of certain motivations, developments, and performances of an individual. The "why's" behind motivations can explain what is causing moment-to-moment decisions for a particular person. The "why's" behind development can give good reasons for the changes needed to be made in a person's abilities. The "why's" behind performances can clarify the rationale for why people do the things they do.

Scientists pose "why" questions in a cause-and-effect form of analysis. We also need to go to a deeper level to understand why some people get stronger (rather than weaker) through adversity, or why one manager fails and another succeeds. As we study Theory *I*, we will go further into "why" questions that get to the heart of what brings about success.

1. Why do some people see opportunities more clearly?
2. Why do some people challenge themselves more regularly?
3. Why do some people seem to have more natural motivation?
4. Why do some people learn more quickly from their mistakes?
5. Why do some people always seem to know what is important to do?

Wrong questions often lead us to more wrong questions. On the surface, the questions we ask may matter to us based upon our feelings about what is right or fair ("What did your manager say that was inappropriate?" or "What did your competitor do that was unscrupulous?" or "How did your spouse act that appeared so cold?"). Questions like these prey upon people's minds. The real issues that impact the motivation, development, and performance of people get lost in rhetoric while important decisions and steps to address opportunities and challenges are ignored. Through Theory *I*, knowing how to demand what you want is replaced with learning how to produce what you want.

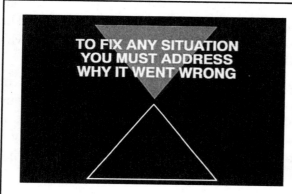

Figure 3

What We Must Do to Fix Any Situation

To fix any situation, we must address why it went wrong (Figure 3). Suppose you bought a new car and were driving it over to a friend's house to show it off. You stop in a gas station to make sure you have enough gas to take your friend out for a drive. You try to start the car, but it won't turn over. You ask the attendant what the problem is. After some testing, the attendant tells you that your battery is dead.

After getting your car jump started, would you simply go to the dealership and have the battery replaced? No, you need to discover why the first battery went dead in the first place. Perhaps the car has some wires crossed. If you simply replaced the battery, sooner or later the battery would die again, because the root problem (the reason for the battery failure) was never corrected.

The types of wires in the car (alternator wires, spark plug wires, headlight wires, etc.) are analogous to the elements we need to examine to fix the problems we face. Each of us needs to know the names of the elements (wires) that are crossed, and why they create problems in particular situations.

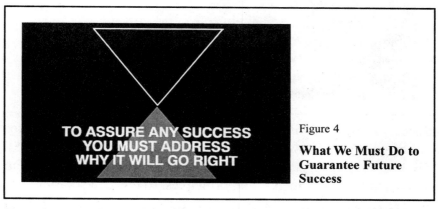

TO ASSURE ANY SUCCESS YOU MUST ADDRESS WHY IT WILL GO RIGHT

Figure 4

What We Must Do to Guarantee Future Success

To assure continued success, we must address why things will go right (Figure 4). Just as there are certain rules or principles we must follow when wiring a car, the same applies to preparing ourselves for producing success in our work. Wires need insulation from cross currents, and we need insulation that separates the negatives from the positives in our lives. While wires and some people appear to be compatible, a quick test can let us know before trouble develops. We can avoid shock by using the right instruments. Theory *I*, through its instruments (tools), helps us understand the real problems and real solutions long before the "sparks" fly.

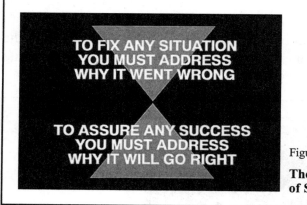

Figure 5

**The Practice
of Success**

Success is the result of combining our understanding of what makes things go wrong as well as what makes things go right (Figure 5). Through the hour-glass effect, problems are broken down into parts, and then reformed, using principles, to create a solution.

The following diagram (Figure 6) represents our initial mind-set (mass of undefined elements, which when discussing a problem can be referred to as symptoms).

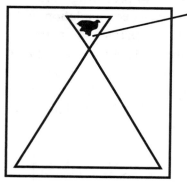

Attitudes can impact us as a result of:

☒ Goals that appear impossible to reach

☒ Relationships that are causing us frustration

☒ Ideologies working against
effective communication

☒ Determinants that diminish
personal commitments

☒ Steps that have been leading us nowhere

Figure 6. **Deconstruction of an Attitude**

Through Theory *I* we will learn five classifications of elements we need to explore for uncovering the real problems in every situation. How we use principles to form these elements into components of a solution, and how we formulate these elements and principles into strategies for implementing solutions (Figure 7) are addressed in this book.

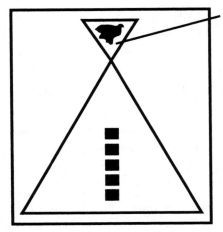

This attitude goes through the hourglass after it is broken down into elements. These elements are properly reformed into new structures using principles.

Every classification of elements is considered and combined through principles to formulate strategies for success:

☒ Select the right goal
☒ Establish the right relationship
☒ Use the right communication ideology
☒ Call upon the right determinants
☒ Take the right steps

Figure 7. **Reconstruction of an Attitude**

The Critical Need for a Methodology

After elements have been sorted, it is necessary to process them. This requires a methodology: a complete system of action that classifies and arranges every critical element and decision for success in a particular situation.

The two most important methodologies in our lives are language and mathematics. Consider the difficulty of learning and using a language where every word is a different symbol, with no reused symbols or rules (principles) for their usage. For instance, the Chinese language contains over 40,000 characters, each representing a distinct idea, thing, or sound. Western languages are a combination of methodologies. We learn our language by understanding our current alphabet (from the Romans in 114 A.D.), by understanding which letters are consonants and which are vowels (originating from the Greeks in 800 B.C.), and the different sounds of each letter (originating from the Phoenicians in 1000 B.C.).

Once we learn the methodology behind our native language, we are able to use diction more wisely, convey meaning more precisely, and demonstrate creative usage more effectively. How different would our lives be today without the benefit of these methodologies?

The lack of a common language typically makes any close cooperation and educational development more difficult. The one-to-one scheme (one character has only one meaning) in the Chinese language made it laborious for the population to learn and prosper. The Chinese government instituted a program to help reduce illiteracy by simplifying more than 2,000 of the over 40,000 Chinese characters. However, this simplification was unsuccessful in boosting literacy because it did not provide a methodology for using even the 2,000 characters. Chinese readers were still held back by an inability to utilize these characters in a productive way.[1]

To create sentences in modern languages, people learn to categorize and place words as nouns, verbs, adverbs, adjectives, pronouns, articles, etc. These become different elements for constructing sentences. There are principles for constructing sentences that assure correct grammar. Learning a methodology allows us to categorize and place bits of information to address new opportunities for success.

In 600 A.D., the Hindus invented a symbol meaning "empty." They drew a circle and put nothing inside, which we now call "zero." By using zero we could move a "1" over one position to represent the number ten. By reusing the nine symbols with zeros and each other, we could count to infinity. There is no limit to our performance in counting because of this methodology. When we dial a phone number, we use a set of numbers based upon ten digits. These same ten digits are used to time our phone calls, present an invoice for phone usage, or write a check in payment. The methodology of numbers allows us to track, monitor, and control our surroundings, rather than face hopeless frustration and allow our surroundings to control us.

In Theory *I*, methodologies are guides that direct performance so that opportunities become more attainable, and challenges become addressable. The more familiar we are with a methodology, the

---

1. *The World Book Encyclopedia*, 1997 ed., s.v. "Literacy," by Harvey Graff.

more benefit we can derive from its use. When a person uses methodologies to act, they can direct and control their own success.

Employees often get up every day simply because they have a responsibility to get to work on time. "Carrot-and-stick" approaches often cause employees to ignore their own genuine interests in being productive, and perhaps slip further below originally defined levels of acceptable performance. Low performers lack a sense of personal control over creating opportunity; they wait for the boss's edict. *"When a man has put a limit on what he will do, he has put a limit on what he can do."* —Charles M. Schwab.

Decisions based on concurrent personal desires and professional needs naturally generate more personal interest in performing your work. Mentally noting your current reasons for going to work establishes a base for building a strategy for future success and personal fulfillment.

Motivation, contrary to popular views, is not about making people work. When a manager hires a motivational consultant to fix a low-morale or low-motivation problem, the consultant typically focuses on various options that: (1) threaten poor behavior (a personalized intimidation form of manipulation), (2) provide more freedom of personal direction and satisfaction (a reward form of manipulation), or (3) build team spirit for increasing the value of joint efforts (a group pressure form of manipulation). We will see later in the book how these three assumptions about motivation ultimately work against effectiveness, particularly in today's complex and competitive working environment.

Motivation results from a methodology that properly defines work in terms that make it appealing, interesting, and meaningful. The gap between what we can do (potential) and what we actually do (performance) can be enormous. To make up for this gap, people over the centuries have tossed around words and phrases, such as courage, bravery, self-reliance, control over self, guts, stamina, discipline, beliefs, proactive attitude, etc. These terms describe what may have "worked" temporarily in forcing new behaviors. However, they are a poor substitute for the tangible steps that must be put in place to direct people to consistent success. We need to formulate a plan that leads us through every decision that will make success happen.

How much damage results from limiting our opportunity? The difference between expectations in our minds and the actual results can be devastating. Some people lower their expectations to their level of proficiency, and accept this as unchangeable. Their perception of attainable opportunity shrinks, and interest, meaning, and encouragement for action evaporate.

When we complain about employees, customers, or self-help books letting us down, where does the problem lie? Who do we blame? Finding blame is not the issue that needs to be explored. Theory *I* helps eliminate pointing out blame by making us look at the three fingers pointing back at us that ask, "What is *our* motivation, development, and performance?

Figure 8. **Winning Requires Continuous Improvement**
Competing effectively requires training and pacing. Our activities should build our capabilities so that we continue to grow.

The need for motivation, development, and performance is clear in the demands placed on us for perfection (Figure 8). No matter how complex the world becomes, people demand satisfaction for their money in nearly everything, from cars, to cable television, to on-line computer networks, to routine medical operations, and literally thousands of other product and service offerings. Astronauts in space depend upon perfection from countless professionals and supporting staff members. Over 7.5 million lines of code must operate flawlessly to launch and guide a space craft for an eight-minute ride into outer space. Scientists can examine phenomena throughout our galaxy and draw conclusions on matters that existed billions of years ago when our galaxy was forming. Top-performing professionals rely upon methodology—a detailed, systematic approach to raising the right questions, uncovering causes of problems, and developing rationale for solutions.

Contrasting Dogma to a Methodology

Dogma is a form of manipulation that destroys personal initiative. We become vulnerable to all sorts of manipulation through a redefinition of our values, such as greed, lust, jealousy, addiction, and other external forces that prey upon our free will and individuality. By supporting weaknesses there is no lasting peace of mind, and this search becomes an endless treadmill for more gratification.

Recently, dogma concerning dedication or company "esprit de corps" has become harmful because it did not prepare workers (who believed their enthusiasm entitled them to job security) for the cut-backs and layoffs that a new economic climate precipitated. Dogma made these people vulnerable and ultimately distressed, financially and emotionally (Figure 9).

A methodology must be used to give new direction and a sense of personal control to those who have suffered distress.

The French naturalist Jean Fabre once observed one-inch long processionary caterpillars that form into long strings and move through trees, eating leaves and insects. At one point, Fabre observed them following each other in an unbroken circle. Fabre thought they would soon realize that they were going around in circles and would stop. Yet, they continued until they starved to death. They did not break the chain to eat some food nearby. These processionary caterpillars are metaphors for people who confuse activity (what people do) with accomplishment (what people receive). People often create "busy-ness" as a substitute for furthering business; they lose sight of key decisions that could direct them to productive activities.

Figure 9. **Losing Control...the Causes and Cures**
What causes people to lose control? When we are manipulated into doing something, we feel as though we have lost control. We become frustrated, and feel we have no recourse. To cure this situation, we must separate ourselves from dogma and embrace a methodology that builds self-reliance.

Many authors on success do not tell you that by providing you with tidbits of incomplete ideas you will increase your dependency upon them for improving yourself. Worse yet, because their approaches leave so much out, your continued failure makes you excessively vulnerable and submissive to their control over your success. Their answer to your struggles is for you to buy more of their wares, because their increased wealth at your expense is proof of their value and your dependency. Their one-time touted success, or their ability to convince others they have *the* answer, is very often unrelated to any transfer of needed knowledge, or the creation of a methodology to meet the requirements at hand. They promise the world, and that feels good. When promises wear off, people often seek another promise. It may temporarily fix the feeling, but these fixes ultimately leave people skeptical, more desperate, and without hope. Promises for success without a methodology destroy individual initiative and control, increase dependency on advisors, and produce stagnant thinking.

Though we might have asked ourselves the right questions at one time, we may have given up along the way because there were no immediate answers. This phenomena begins in childhood when we want to know why certain things happened. Busy parents often reply, "Because that's just the way it is," or "Because I said so." We quickly learn to stop asking such "stupid questions!" We see authority as central to the answers we sought, whether they were good or bad. We may stop asking the important questions because they became more annoying than helpful.

Before learning the Theory *I* methodology, we waste time pondering and agonizing over "why" questions that stay at the surface of what impacts us personally. "Why is my boss angry with me?" "Why didn't my client buy the product or service?" "Why is my spouse always finding fault with me?" "Why is my child not interested in attending college?" "Why am I not more successful at this point in my life?" "Why don't I do what I know can make me successful?" Growing lists of questions like these add complexity and confusion. Worse yet, superimposing highly touted grand principles of dogma creates expectations that make matters far more difficult. This could take the form of advice, like telling a manager to show patience, or telling a salesperson to give the customer whatever the customer wants. A whole new set of needless responses (like guilt, remorse, or fear) are created, needlessly frustrating the individual.

Surprisingly, motivational "experts" openly admit their approaches do not work at all for some people. "Some of you will not improve," they warn, "while others of you will become successful." What these "flavor of the month" authors and speakers fail to tell you is that, by simply focusing on what you are doing, or by trying something different, your chances for success increase. If 100 people were told their performances would improve by using a different pen every day of the week, a certain percentage of them would improve. And these people would give convincing testimonies to that improvement. The Hawthorne studies documented this phenomenon between 1927 and 1932 at the Western Electric Company by proving that whether lighting was increased or later decreased, productivity went up. This productivity increase was not due to the lighting, but rather to the workers' reaction to all of the attention from the experiment. These workers, treated as if they were important and unique, felt they had a major voice in deciding on the management of their own time, and were insulated (inadvertently by the researchers) from the routine demands and restrictions of management.

Motivation Versus Manipulation

Manipulation can cause stress and frustration with no end in sight. Manipulation preys on a person's weaknesses and frailties. Motivation is a positive force that puts a person in greater control over themselves while at the same time building upon inner strength. Motivation is always good for people. Manipulation is a negative force that puts one person in control over another person while increasing weaknesses and encouraging dependency.

Manipulation, which may lead to temporary success, ultimately works against people's development because it makes people dependent upon external controls. That success rewards manipulators, thus perpetuating their management style of external control. The effect of this perpetuation becomes evident when new circumstances arise and the people who are under external control (who lack the internal control for self-motivation) are unable to engage in any new opportunity. Those people, as well as the manipulators, are left behind by those who are self-motivated for success.

We have all had goals that press on our minds from time to time. The culmination of this could be a "success nightmare." Let's suppose you wake up in the middle of the night startled for no apparent reason. You lay there and begin thinking about what has been worrying you lately.

You begin thinking to yourself, "If only I could uncover the barrier to solving the problem, I could turn this problem into a success."

Dogma may come to mind as a guide or solution. You begin combing through generic suggestions or slogans in hopes of finding an answer: "Believe in yourself!" and "If it is to be, it is up to me," etc. All of these tips frustrate you even more because they do not offer you concrete steps to solving the problem.

You may ask yourself, "How do I get started? What's the first step? How can I use these seemingly good ideas and 'believe in myself' when things are not going well?" To be effective we need tools that lead us to the causes of the problems and the steps to a solution. Theory I increases our sensitivities to the variables that bring about success. We can learn bits and pieces from other people; however, the entire plan must ultimately be developed and executed from within each one of us. We need to learn about the tools that create success within a comprehensive methodology.

If you currently use an approach that leaves you wondering, "What should I do first?" or "Once I get started, I get lost and don't know what to do next," or "I can never be sure I am making progress," or "I am not exactly clear on what the real problem is, so I can't formulate the most appropriate solution," then you are ready for Theory I, where these and many more questions are answered specifically and from within ourselves.

People differ in their motivation, development, and performance. To what can we attribute success, mediocrity, or failure? At the foundation of all sciences is the notion of cause and effect. In Theory I the cause is the attribute, and the effect is the goal, relationship, ideology, determinant, or step. Later in the book we will attach each attribute to a corresponding element to better understand how we can become accountable for defining the problem and the solution from within ourselves.

Figure 10. **The Stress We Enjoy**
We have all been euphoric from riding on a roller coaster. This exaggerated feeling is an escape from reality that does not threaten our well-being. We are exhilarated by the experience, not fearful.

Motivation forms *eustress*, a positive form of stress that increases motivation, enhances development, and improves performance. During motivation a person's blood chemistry changes in such a manner that they feel better, enjoy what they are doing, think more clearly, do better work, remain healthier, and live longer.[2]

An example of eustress: When a person wearing a parachute willingly jumps out of an airplane and pulls the "D" ring followed by the chute opening, they experience a rush of emotion and energy that is exhilarating. While floating through the air gazing at the sky and earth below, they experience eustress (Figure 10).

Manipulation forms distress, a negative form of stress that initially heightens intensity while decreasing a sense of individual motivation. Manipulation ultimately diminishes proper development and lowers effective performance. During manipulation a person's blood

2. Richard Restak, M. D., *The Brain* (New York: Bantam Books, 1984), 165.

chemistry changes in such a manner that they feel worse, experience less enjoyment in what they are doing, become confused and even disoriented more easily, do poorer work, become sick, and lead a shorter life.[3] Addictive behavior may result from attempts to counteract distress by changing blood chemistry. However, the false sense of well-being created by addictive behavior most commonly leads to greater distress.

An example of distress: When a person wearing a parachute willingly jumps out of an airplane and pulls the "D" ring, and the handle comes off, the chute does not open, and the person and the closed chute begin plummeting toward the earth at a terminal velocity between 120 to 180 miles per hour. The person frantically looks for the other handle. Panic creates mental barriers, so even the most necessary of actions become difficult to execute.

Many people today are looking for another "handle" to take control over their lives. With all of the changes occurring in the job market, finding "handles" for getting a new job is difficult for people lacking a methodology. People become highly frustrated and sense a lack of direction and control as the doors to success become obscure behind the vastness and complexity of new opportunities. People seeking to grasp the handles for what directs, controls, and provides access to new visions and steps for fulfillment need an interrelated table of elements to unlock the doors to success.

Theory *I*'s perspective allows us to balance emotions and logic. Emotions can often fixate us in the right sides of our brains, while logic becomes irrelevant for the moment. Later, after the emotions subside and the reality of failure sets in, we question through the left sides of our brains, "What are the real answers that ensure success? Do they exist?" With an all-encompassing strategy, the answer is clearly, "Yes!"

The keys to success: Who has them for you? No one! How can you find them? You can't! Keys to success are not found. They are created

---

3. Ibid.

out of elements just as recipes use different ingredients to make your favorite dishes.

How can we seize any opportunity and make it produce for us? Managers need to pursue opportunities for employees to contribute skills and efforts to accomplish objectives. Salespeople need to pursue opportunities to gain agreements with potential customers to buy products and services. These stated needs are based upon elements within Theory *I*. We will begin exploring these elements in chapter 3.

Elements as the Building Blocks to Success

We need to break down each opportunity into useable and formulable pieces called elements. During our most difficult encounters we need an ability to uncover the elements at work in the particular situation we face. The benefit of breaking down (atomizing) our challenges into elements is illustrated in the "Rime of the Ancient Mariner" by Samuel Taylor Coleridge:

> *Water, water, every where,*
> *And all the boards did shrink;*
> *Water, water, every where,*
> *Nor any drop to drink.*

Baking in the hot sun, an old man lost at sea is about to die, lacking water to drink. Opportunity, like water, is something all of us need to survive. If the old man had the ability to break salt water down into H_2O and $NaCl$ (two separate elements), he could survive much longer and perhaps make it to shore. Our bodies need water and salt (principles of life); however, too much salt water can make us delirious, like too much undifferentiated opportunity. The mariner needs a survival plan (strategy) to get to shore, using water and salt separately. When we become disoriented and confused (cannot separate out the elements, understand the functioning principles, or construct the essential strategies for success), we lose sight of our opportunities. We have less reason for getting up in the morning.

Since opportunity is so important, why is it that we know so little about how it fits into our own methodology for success? "Think positive" is good advice from Norman Vincent Peale's 1952 top-selling book on success, *The Power of Positive Thinking*; however, do we know what elements to consider in order to generate positive results? Do we even know how to think clearly?

Coleridge published his poem in 1798. Perhaps today he would write:

> *Opportunity, opportunity, every where,*
> *And all the companies did shrink;*
> *Opportunity, opportunity every where,*
> *Nor anyone to think.*

We have heard, "You can lead a horse to water, but you can't make it drink." Does that mean we should stop leading horses to water? Horses (ourselves) need water (opportunity) to survive. Before "leading a horse to water" we need to know about the horse's health and the condition of the water. A dogmatic approach insists upon the horse drinking and ignores the potential causes of problems or consequences. For instance, if employees were not working up to standard, a dogmatic boss would force them to work, regardless of any other factors preventing them from functioning at full capacity. The dogmatic boss might assume that the employees' failure is the result of an "attitude problem." When we dismiss problems as a result of "attitude," we have given more credence to symptoms than problems. Who loses? The employee obviously, but also the employer in lost productivity, feedback on real problems, creative input in the workplace, and replacement training time. If we are serious about success, we need to take a scientific approach that leads us to real problems and real solutions.

For example, Ross, a neighbor of mine, sells investments. He tells me he studied a motivational approach that encourages asking at least one person per day for a lead through a friend, associate, or client. "With an ocean of opportunity in the world, why restrict yourself to one drop at a time?" I asked. Ross's success had become dependent upon a drip-by-drip approach to becoming successful.

Theory *I* helped Ross get to the root of the real problem. His lack of confidence stemmed from two circumstances. First, he was afraid to ask for a favor that might fracture his relationship with his client or his client's relationship with the referenced person. Second, he did not know how to create leads through conversation. Ross's goal was, "To contact one person each day and ask for one lead." This is a goal of performance—making the call and asking the question. This goal has no measure of success other than going through the motions. Forcing someone to act without understanding the real problem and solution creates potential for disasters.

A Theory *I* goal would be based upon specific facts about Ross, the client, and the situation. To learn more about Ross, the client, and the situation, Theory *I* offers Opportunity/Challenge Surveys to identify the real challenges Ross faces.

One potential Theory *I* solution might read, "Ross needs to have a goal of development that teaches him the circumstances under which he should request leads with respect to: (1) Context within the services just rendered, (2) Comments from the client that represent openness to such a request, and (3) Statements from Ross that could elicit appropriate signals from his client."

Without Theory *I*, Ross may approach the most inappropriate person in his client list and unintentionally dissolve his relationship and future business potential. This in turn may turn Ross off to prospecting; or worse yet, Ross may lose confidence and begin calling fewer clients to avoid either the prospect of problems or the problem of prospects. We need to select our opportunities based upon potential and performance. Ross's performance is limited due to ignorance, hesitancy, insecurity, and inability. Theory *I* bridges the gap between potential (what is possible) and performance (what Ross can do now) through a strategy for learning how to obtain a reference. (Please see the Theory *I* Foundation for Success diagram, page 2.) The drip-by-drip approach has minimal performance requirements, creating an unnecessary bottleneck and limitation on Ross's capabilities and opportunities.

Ross needed specific facts and ideas to meet *his* challenge, not general challenges. There has never been a comprehensive, properly structured language for integrating all success. Communication courses and structured sales calls attempt to construct tidbits of information to meet stated objectives. Personality tests categorize people in relation to certain descriptive traits deemed most important by the test designers. All of these assessments hope to create certain effects and produce personal understanding while avoiding conflict and satisfying the narrow objectives of the test designers. While the assessments may achieve limited improved personal understanding, they are not comprehensive or applicable to every situation and therefore fall short of producing repeatable success. They focus on their own contrived and limited expectations, rather than a methodology for reaching potential.

Good ideas and confidence about building success are not enough. Henry Ford said, "If you think you can or can't, you are always right." Henry Ford thought he could become highly successful, and he did. Other people throughout history thought they would become successful, and they did. The other side of this statement is often ignored. Many people thought they were going to become successful and did not. Casinos and lotteries could not exist without people adopting Henry Ford's pattern of thinking. In other words, false hopes are easily encouraged by impossible promises. Ford's doctrine does not assure success because it begins and ends with pure hope. There are no supporting elements, principles, or strategies to make it happen.

The possibilities for inappropriate decisions and failure increase as the number of variables impacting success increase. In the midst of confusion we may seek a doctrine that sounds enticing. *"The question is not whether a doctrine is beautiful but whether it is true. When we wish to go to a place, we do not ask whether the road leads through a pretty country, but whether it is the right road."* —Hare. Doctrine is institutionalized dogma that represents a fixed pattern of steps that begins with fixed answers; methodology is an investigative approach that leads to the best answer. There are choices we need to make when seeking our potential to success. We can either allow outside factors to control us, or we can develop a stronger force within ourselves to provide our own guidance. The difference between high expectations and low performance is disappointment. We can reverse that relationship, and ensure our fulfillment by exceeding those expectations

CHAPTER 2

THE CONCEPTS AND TERMINOLOGY OF THEORY *I*

We lay the groundwork for producing success by addressing **The Basis of the Theory *I* Methodology** and **The Terminology of Theory *I***. We broaden our perspective on success through an **Introduction to the Theory *I* Element Chart and Table of Success Elements**. To learn how to use this new knowledge, we examine **The Five Characteristics of the Theory *I* Elements, Parallel Strategies Using GRIDS, The Formation of the Principles of Success, The Science Behind Theory *I*, The Theory *I* Element Chart**, and **The Table of Success Elements**.

The Basis of the Theory *I* Methodology

Theory *I* has the following characteristics: There is nothing to memorize. There are no lists of suggestions to follow. There will be no comparisons of your work with the work of anyone else. You will not be expected to mimic other people's styles or approaches. There is absolutely no fear of failure because your chance of success is 100 percent. Theory *I* has the precision of mathematics, the flexibility of a modern language, and the thoroughness of a scientific methodology.

Theory *I* uses a scientific approach beginning with (a) *elements* that specifically define what affects the essentials for certain success (motivation, development, and performance), (b) *principles* that guide the successful combining of all these elements, and (c) *strategies* that provide a systematic application for pursuing unlimited opportunities and challenges. All of the necessary tools are provided to ensure your approach is effectively implemented.

What unique, specific focus does each individual need to create success? Theory *I* considers all potential variables (using elements noted in The Theory *I* Element Chart at the end of the chapter).

Gathering the gems of wisdom we need for an opportunity or challenge is not always easy because we do not know for certain where to look. If I were to tell you about a garden with a path that led you near 25 small rocks, each covering a piece (each element) of a map leading to diamonds in a mine, how many rocks would you lift? "All of them!" is the most common answer, to complete the map (strategy). To complete a readable map, each piece must be face-up and adjacent to connecting pieces (principle). In Theory *I* there are 25 elements we need to uncover and examine for mapping our path to success.

There are two tools of Theory *I* used for exploring and applying elements to any situation:

1. **Opportunity/Challenge Surveys (OCS)** help us comb through 25 elements at a time to identify the key elements for addressing relevant problems and issues regarding personal and corporate success. The survey addresses all critical barriers by using selected elements as the foundation for building an effective strategy.

2. **Table of Success Elements (TSE)** is a 5 element by 5 element classification table that helps us combine individual elements, principles, and strategies into a comprehensive, properly sequenced series of strategies (a superstrategy) using the Theory *I* methodology.

Rather than tell anyone how to succeed, Theory *I* provides these tools for each of us to explain to ourselves about how we will succeed in our own particular way. Theory *I* Axiom: Through the use of a complete methodology, all failures, feedback, analysis, and adjustments become part of an evolutionary process toward producing success. Human factors are present in every successful situation.

When things go well, what should we examine to repeat that success? If things do not go well, what should we examine for improvement or development? Initially, it is easier to appreciate the results of success, rather than the causes. In the long run, focusing on the causes reveals that there are three essentials for success: persistence in motivation, conscientiousness in development, and accountability in performance.

Inherent self-direction, logic, and an internal building process strengthen people. The Theory *I* methodology enables unlimited applications which result in unbridled enthusiasm for continued development and performance. Awareness of needed development is encouraged through meaningful feedback. Adjustments are very much a part of everything we do in Theory *I*. Performance becomes far more predictable and controllable, so we become more accountable for undeniable success (Figure 11).

Figure 11. **Human Factors and Immense Challenges**
To climb to new heights we must face the elements. *Elements* can work in our favor if we understand how they work and how to take full advantage of them. Guidelines founded upon *principles* help ensure our safe journey. *Strategies* lead us on solid footing toward our destination.

Elements are the smallest entity we need to consider and address. They are grouped into five classes with five elements each. Principles are formed to govern the combining of these elements. Strategies become specific responses to these elements for addressing a particular situation.

In the following two diagrams (Figures 12 and 13) from left to right, we first see the block in the top triangle (defined in a previous diagram with the word ATTITUDE) being broken down into pieces that pass through the hour glass to the bottom triangle. In the second diagram we see two columns of these smaller blocks (elements) that represent two strategies. Please note that two of the elements are shared between the strategies.

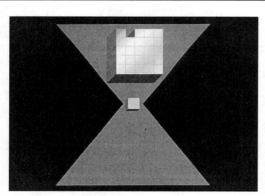

Figure 12
Beginnning with Elements

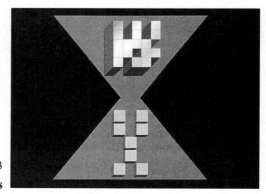

Figure 13
Ending with Strategies

THE TERMINOLOGY OF THEORY *I*

1. Element name is the word listed in italics under the heading ELEMENTS in the Theory *I* Element Chart, and in the Table of Success Elements at the top of each cell. There are five elements per class. Example: *accomplishment* = the first element in the Primary Goal class.

2. Class is one of five horizontal categories of elements in the Table of Success Elements. Example: Primary Goals = a Class. Basic Relationships = a Class, and so on. Each different Class provokes a more thorough and unique inquiry. Example: The Primary Goal Class answers the question, "Which results assure success?" (More on this in chapter 3).

3. Class number or C# is an ordination number that is a point of reference for each element within the respective class. Example: G1 = C# for *accomplishment*. This number ties together each of the tools of Theory *I*: The Table of Success Elements and The Opportunity/Challenge Survey.

4. Attributes for each element are words in bold type in the Theory *I* Element Chart, and directly beneath the element in the Table of Success Elements. By focusing on an attribute, that element will ultimately be satisfied. Example: **Maximizing Effectiveness** is the attribute that will bring about the element of *accomplishment*.

5. Key element question is immediately beneath the C# in the Table of Success Elements only and is used to decide if the particular element applies for a particular challenge or opportunity. Example: For *accomplishment*, the key element question is: "Are all routine tasks performed at the expected/required level of proficiency?" When elements are so selected to address a particular situation, they become key elements that participate in resolving the situation at hand.

Introduction to the Theory *I* Element Chart and Table of Success Elements

The Theory *I* elements are listed in the Theory *I* Element Chart at the end of this chapter. Everything we learn about and do related to Theory *I* has a foundation built upon the elements defined in this chart. These elements grow in significance as they become connected to each other through the entire Theory *I* methodology.

Just as the value of using language or mathematics continues to increase through daily usage, so does the Theory *I* methodology. Because any element(s) can join any other element(s) in the chart to describe a problem (inappropriate combination) or produce a solution (appropriate combination), the number of combinations that explain barriers or paths to success is 1.55×10^{25} or 15,500,000,000,000,000,000,000,000. The potential number of combinations this new methodology provides for analysis, understanding, and solutions is a number larger than the estimated more than 10 billion trillion stars in the universe or 1.0×10^{23}. While the combinations may seem infinite, choosing them is simplified by using Theory *I*.

When we embark on a journey to fulfill an opportunity or to satisfy a challenge, we need to select goals that will properly direct our attention. Goals describe our destination or end result; however, they are not the end result. For example, we may want our football team to win a championship: a desirable end result. To win the championship we need to achieve the winning of more games than any other team. To win each game we need more points than the opposition. Points in football are earned by the reaching of goals through field goals or touchdowns. Reaching either of these goals in the form of *achievements* for first-time attainments, or *accomplishments* for routine attainments, can lead us to the desirable end result of winning the championship. Going for the wrong goal or the right goal at the wrong time may cause us to lose the game, and ultimately, the championship. Going a step further, besides helping us select the right goal, Theory *I* helps us focus on the right attribute that will guide us toward reaching the right goal. Later in the book we will see examples of how wrong business goals lead to failure.

Each of the Primary Goals is an element because there is a finite number of five goals that cannot be divided or increased in number. Knowing when to seek each of these five Primary Goals leads us to a particular attainment that contributes to the end result. People often confuse goals, results, and attributes for success. By not knowing the difference, people may focus on what causes failure. Many would-be Olympic champions have focused on the gold medal and never received one. The gold medal is the desired end result. The goal is to produce a performance worthy of earning a gold medal. What does a gold medal have to do with becoming a gold medalist? The size, the weight, the color, or the shape, have nothing to do with gymnastics, diving, swimming, weight lifting, soccer, etc. Then why would athletes spend even a split second thinking about these characteristics? Because that is precisely what they want. The same applies to executives focused on their own prestige, salespeople focused on commissions, or researchers focused on a special award. The focus needs to be on the attributes of a top performer, not the reward received by a top performer.

To discover what made a person successful, we need to know about their focuses and decisions. An ideal opening question regarding past failures or successes may be, "What were you thinking about during your performance?" and "What decisions did you make regarding your goals, relationships, ideologies, determinants, and steps (GRIDS)?" What is on a person's mind and the decisions they make with reference to GRIDS leads them to success or failure. Theory *I* deepens the question with, "To what do you attribute your motivation, development, and performance?" Attributes make the difference.

Within the Theory *I* methodology there are attributes for each of the five Primary Goals, as well as the elements in every other class (GRIDS) that make up this theory. Attributes are what we focus on to make the right things happen or to produce the long-term desired results. Again, these attributes (defined in the previous section, the Terminology of Theory *I*) are introduced in the Theory *I* Element Chart and are further illustrated in the Table of Success Elements. (Both are found at the end of this chapter.)

In summary, the Theory *I* Element Chart offers an overall perspective of all the elements and their respective attributes within Theory *I*. The Table of Success Elements formats this Element Chart into a matrix where there are five classes of elements. They are grouped as follows:

The Five Classes of Theory *I* Elements
GRIDS

1. Primary Goals   (G1 - G5)

2. Basic Relationships   (R1 - R5)

3. Principal Ideologies   (I1 - I5)

4. Prime Determinants   (D1 - D5)

5. Fundamental Steps   (S1 - S5)

The Theory *I* Element Chart provides a simple introduction and some familiarity with each of the elements and attributes. Beginning with the first element, we read this chart as follows:

"To satisfy the element of [*accomplishment*] we focus on the attribute and tasks that address [**maximizing effectiveness**, so people can become more proficient in completing required routine work on time.]"

The class number for the first element, *accomplishment*, is "G1" or the first Primary Goal.

Success is the result of combining the right goal with the right relationship. In set theory terminology, goals are an *equivalent set* with relationships. This simply means a particular goal (*accomplishment*) can join only a particular relationship (*management*) and vice versa. This set theory rule is shown by the corresponding cells of the top two rows of the matrix (The Table of Success Elements).

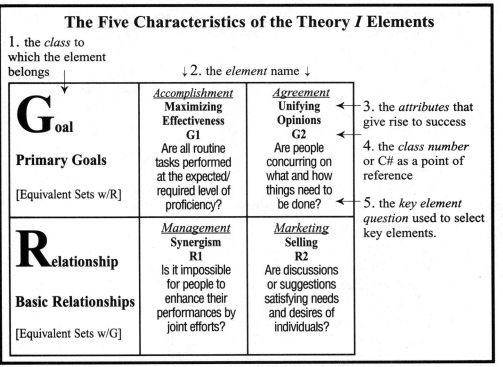

The Five Characteristics of the Theory *I* Elements

1. the *class* to which the element belongs

↓ 2. the *element* name ↓

Goal **Primary Goals** [Equivalent Sets w/R]	*Accomplishment* **Maximizing Effectiveness** **G1** Are all routine tasks performed at the expected/required level of proficiency?	*Agreement* **Unifying Opinions** **G2** Are people concurring on what and how things need to be done?
Relationship **Basic Relationships** [Equivalent Sets w/G]	*Management* **Synergism** **R1** Is it impossible for people to enhance their performances by joint efforts?	*Marketing* **Selling** **R2** Are discussions or suggestions satisfying needs and desires of individuals?

3. the *attributes* that give rise to success

4. the *class number* or C# as a point of reference

5. the *key element question* used to select key elements.

The Table of Success Elements (the matrix version of the Theory *I* Element Chart) will be expanded throughout the book, as its usefulness to us increases. As we progress through the book we will see our involvement in our success increase.

For example: We become involved in a project or a job when we decide we want a certain result. Once this is decided, we need to select a goal to lead us to that result. After selecting a goal we need to select a relationship to support that goal, and this greater-involvement process continues as we go further down the matrix.

As we increase our participation we increase our success. A goal without a relationship is merely a pipe dream. Pipe dreams are at the zero level of success because there are no results, no progress, and no serious expectations for any change in reality. In each of the following chapters we will see how each level of GRIDS maps out our journey to success.

The properties of the Table of Success Elements include all elements pertaining to success that were introduced in the Theory *I* Element Chart. The structure and flow of the Table is as follows: From top to bottom, a person using this table will increase their participation in the success being considered. As their participation increases, so does their success along the way.

When a person is capable of performing certain tasks, the left side of the Table applies (Performance). When a person is not capable of performing certain tasks, the right side of the Table applies (Development). There is a corresponding progression for all elements between these two positions in the table.

With a desired result in mind, we progress down the table from Primary Goal to Basic Relationship elements. Participation and ability for creating a path to that end result increases. Mapping our way to success requires considering the entire Table or GRIDS. In standard maps we need coordinates to locate where we are and where we are headed. Theory *I*'s GRIDS coordinates where we need to go based on where we are and what is possible.

Parallel Strategies Using GRIDS

The USAF annual quality program featured a presentation on Theory *I* and GRIDS in October 1994. Prior to the program, a half-day briefing from Col. John Warden III, creator of the Gulf War strategy, revealed a commonality between his highly successful parallel strategy of the Gulf War and Theory *I*'s parallel strategies for all success.

Winning wars requires maps, and maps require coordinates or grids for planning and communicating strategies. Rather than the slow, ineffective *serial* strategy used for years in the Vietnam War, the highly successful attack used by the United States in the Gulf War followed a *parallel* strategy approach. In order to gather the information needed to define all significant targets (communications sites, sources of electricity, etc.), comprehensive reconnaissance missions revealing all vulnerabilities were completed before the attack began.

Once the decision to attack these defined targets was made, it was time to develop a superstrategy. *Superstrategy* is a term created for Theory *I* to describe a comprehensive, interrelated, synergistic strategy satisfying a series of orchestrated supporting strategies. Superstrategies are specifically designed to produce results that far exceed all expectations of participants within a given situation.

Parts of the superstrategy in the Gulf War included (1) selecting the best weapons, (2) appropriately selecting and rehearsing trained personnel to carry out the mission, and (3) waiting for the most ideal conditions in which to implement the attack. Once each of these criteria was considered, the parallel strategies of the war could be properly sequenced and implemented with the greatest chance of success.

Simultaneously, all critically important targets for enemy communications and electricity had been hit within the first 24 hours, making development of effective counter strategies virtually impossible. Highly keen and accurate usage of combined air and ground forces created an undeniable march toward victory with very little hesitation or resistance. Technology allowed the United States to use precision in attacking specific targets. Most of us remember seeing bombs being fed down smoke stacks in Iraq.

The U.S. did not complete its mission as a result of luck. There is an identifiable matrix to success in the battlefield, and this type of matrix can be applied to attaining goals in the office. The highly keen and accurate parallel strategies generated through Theory *I* produce our own personal and team victories.

Many of us are not sure what needs changing to increase our effectiveness. The first problem we need to avoid is changing decisions that were correct! It is common for people to select the wrong goal and become frustrated. Secondly, they may select the wrong relationship to support that goal. Frustration increases. Thirdly, they may select an ideology or communication style that forces people to respond to the problem. The result may be a missed goal, a destroyed relationship, and a group of people who continue to fail and make matters worse!

There are victories that await us for *accomplishments*, *agreements*, *achievements*, and much more. Through Theory *I* we form parallel strategies that simultaneously investigate and employ every element affecting each of these areas. Parallel strategies help us identify the key elements in any situation. We learn to orchestrate all of these strategies so they do not conflict, but rather support each other as a superstrategy. A superstrategy can be placed into effect only after we identify all of the key elements and have configured them into strategies using the Table of Success Elements.

All success is the result of something that first happens inside each one of us. Many people tell us many things, but that which we absorb, understand, and ultimately use is what really makes the difference. Success is the result of what we do, not simply what we are told; therefore, if we are to create success, we need strategies that capitalize on most fully using our capabilities in a direction that makes success happen. To initiate that direction we need principles.

The Formation of the Principles of Success

Principles govern the rules for combining elements. For example, within the classification of Primary Goals, a goal of *accomplishment* is clearly not a goal of *agreement*. One principle to be gleaned from this fact is: *Accomplishments* can be attained with or without *agreements*. The most productive and valuable employees may disagree with *management* on a number of issues. If *managers* will put on a *marketing* "hat" and ask the employees why they disagree, both sides may learn something of value.

Principles guide us in the formation of powerful combinations, such as joining Primary Goal elements to certain Basic Relationship elements. Underlying these principles are the rules of *set theory*. Set theory is a branch of mathematics that deals with relations between sets (as represented by boxes or *cells* in the Table of Success Elements). The applicable rules of set theory will be explained by showing the vertical and horizontal connections of cells in later chapters.

The Science Behind Theory *I*

Theory *I*'s scientific methodology is a way of thinking about and solving problems. The steps for using a scientific methodology vary between scientists but generally include the following:

        a. Stating the Problem
        b. Forming the Hypothesis
        c. Observing and Experimenting
        d. Interpreting the Data
        e. Drawing Conclusions

We need a scientific methodology for success because we must (1) ensure thoroughness in coverage (elements) to sort through the numerous tidbits of suggestions being offered, (2) remain headed in the right direction (principles) to avoid unnecessary mistakes while making wise decisions along the way, and (3) make success formulable (with a strategy) to assure success, rather than leaving success up to a matter of aimless trial and error (or fate).

Theory *I* satisfies the scientific methodology by stating problems in terms of elements, forming hypotheses through a theory for our individual and corporate success, providing the foundation for observing, experimenting, interpreting data, and drawing conclusions through the Table of Success Elements.

Now, let's examine Goals and Relationships further.

The Theory *I* Element Chart

ELEMENTS by Class (C#) join **ATTRIBUTES** to support the performance of **CRITICAL TASKS**

C#	ELEMENTS	ATTRIBUTES SUPPORTING CRITICAL TASKS
To satisfy the element of...↓		...we focus on the attribute and tasks that address...↓
G1	accomplishment	...**maximizing effectiveness**, so people can become more proficient in completing required routine work on time.
G2	agreement	... **unifying opinions**, so people can learn to appreciate and accept proposed ideas, products, or services.
G3	affiliation	...**forming bonds**, so people can create a much closer knit, mutually reassuring, and more highly supportive group.
G4	affirmation	...**confirming wholeness**, so people can build inner strength with a sense of greater self-worth and well-being that promotes confidence.
G5	achievement	...**ensuring growth**, so people can learn new capabilities for competing and contributing new and more significant efforts.
R1	management	...**synergizing** the talents and efforts of people, so they can effectively cooperate and work in concert with others.
R2	marketing	...**selling** features, advantages, and benefits of ideas, products, or services, so other people can appreciate their value.
R3	matching	...**sharing** complementary personal strengths and weaknesses, so people can offset limitations and appreciate teams and individuals.
R4	ministry	... **serving** others to expand their self-assurance, self-respect, and self-confidence, so people can continually become more productive.
R5	mastery	...**skills** for maturation of important, new capabilities, so people can contribute to themselves, others, and the organization.
I1	Theory *X*	...**commands**, so people can insist upon complete compliance in meeting all demands for specifically defined results.
I2	Theory *Y*	...**camaraderie**, so people's efforts are based upon more personal freedoms and satisfaction with low outside interference or control.
I3	Theory *Z*	...**consensus**, so people can foster cooperation and joint efforts through a more congenial, coordinated, community effort.
I4	Theory *M*	...**confusion** to rouse people, so they become more self-directed and inner reliant to control the effects of supervised upsets or disruptions.
I5	Theory *I*	...**competencies**, so people can produce new capabilities to satisfy growing needs for fulfillment and unprecedented competitive demands.
D1	instructions	...**health directives**, so people can properly undertake physical conditioning to get in shape through diet, exercise, and rest.
D2	instincts	...**natural tendencies**, so people can generate competitive, vigorous exertions to push themselves further in giving their strongest efforts.
D3	information	...**facts and beliefs**, so people can test the pro's and con's of specifically what is required for people to become highly successful.
D4	imagination	...**hopes and dreams**, so people can seriously consider, pursue, visualize, and mentally prepare to do exactly what is required of them.
D5	individuality	...**self-determination**, so people can decide to do whatever it takes to succeed while drawing upon all of their inner strength.
S1	environment	...**opportunities**, so people can see where success can occur at all levels from the most easily explored and exploited to the most difficult.
S2	experience	...**challenge**, so people will become personally involved and will directly sense the real, dramatic needs for producing success.
S3	elements	...**theory**, so people can examine all factors and identify those that willl play a role in assuring personal/corporate successs in a given situation.
S4	exercises	...**activities**, so people can practice precisely what will build their abilities and perspectives in preparing for the most assured success.
S5	experiments	...**to-do's**, so people can explicitly define and execute every step toward understanding and effectiveness that produces success.

THE TABLE OF SUCCESS ELEMENTS
WITH KEY ELEMENT QUESTIONS
("No" responses indicate key elements.)

Increasing Participation ←Performance....................Balance....................Development→

	Accomplishment **Maximizing Effectiveness** G1	*Agreement* **Unifying Opinions** G2	*Affiliation* **Forming Bonds** G3	*Affirmation* **Confirming Wholeness** G4	*Achievement* **Ensuring Growth** G5
Goal **Primary Goals** [Equivalent Sets w/R]	Are all routine tasks performed at the expected/ required level of proficiency?	Are people concurring on what and how things need to be done?	Are people working closely together while supporting the overall efforts?	Are people supported in easing burdens and meeting personal needs?	Are people developing new abilities to do what they need to do?
	Management **Synergism** R1	*Marketing* **Selling** R2	*Matching* **Sharing** R3	*Ministry* **Serving** R4	*Mastery* **Skills** R5
Relationship **Basic Relationships** [Equivalent Sets w/G]	Is it impossible for people to enhance their performances by joint efforts?	Are discussions or suggestions satisfying needs and desires of individuals?	Do people's strengths balance and complement each other?	Do people lend support to other people needing self-assurance and direction?	Are people consistently developing their expertise for effectiveness?
	Theory X **Command** I1	*Theory Y* **Camaraderie** I2	*Theory Z* **Consensus** I3	*Theory M* **Confusion** I4	*Theory I* **Competency** I5
Ideology **Principal Ideologies** [Subsets of Theory I]	Do people know what to do and how to do it without being told to perform?	Do people have the freedom to do what is most meaningful and gratifying?	Do people work cooperatively in support of one another as an effective team?	When people feel job security, do they strive to increase their effectiveness?	Are people fulfilled while developing expertise to be most effective?
	Instructions **Health Directives** D1	*Instincts* **Natural Tendencies** D2	*Information* **Facts and Beliefs** D3	*Imagination* **Hopes and Dreams** D4	*Individuality* **Self-Determination** D5
Determinant **Prime Determinants** [Overlapping Sets]	Are people physically capable and mentally alert for performing?	Do people sense the probability of themselves clearly attaining success?	Do people know enough about the expected tasks to ensure success?	Can people see the possibilities for new results to create more success?	Are people capable of developing their own fulfillment within success?
	Environment **Opportunities—** Where Success Is Possible S1	*Experience* **Challenge—** Where Need for Success Is Felt S2	*Elements* **Theory—** Where Success Is Born S3	*Exercises* **Activities—** Where Success Is Nurtured S4	*Experiments* **To-Do's—** Where Success Happens S5
Step **Fundamental Steps** [Universal Sets]	Do people take the simplest route first, to increase their chances for successful performances?	Do people feel they are an important part of what needs to be done to create success?	Do people have a perspective for success that is built upon even the smallest key variables?	Are people receiving the needed feedback and practice for fine-tuning success?	Are people able to develop a strategy for mapping their potential to success?

CHAPTER 3

GOALS AND RELATIONSHIPS

We start our journey to success by addressing: **Goals as Guides for Success; The Need for The Five Primary Goals; Introducing the First Classification of Elements—The Primary Goals; Procedures for Using the Table of Success Elements; Primary Goals, Attributes, and Key Element Questions;** and, **Basic Relationships, Attributes, and Key Element Questions.**

Goals as Guides for Success

Success is the end result of reaching a goal. End results may be a certain level of profit for a company, winning a contract with a particular client, having a meaningful personal relationship with a special person, helping another person succeed, or developing a new capability for yourself.

It is common for people to think they need to focus on the end result. However, it is the goal, not the end result, that properly leads us to success. The entire GRIDS matrix is a map guiding us toward attaining that end result. Too often people describe goals in terms of end results. End results are what people want: money, prestige, medals, championships, enjoyment, fulfillment, or meaningful work. These are not goals, but rather the result of successfully reaching goals. As we will see later, this distinction becomes extremely important when creating a mind-set for success. We don't get rich thinking about money. We don't win awards thinking about medals. Each of us needs to use Theory *I* to select unique and personal goals to lead us to our own successes; these selections increase our commitment and abilities for reaching those goals.

Figure 14

Stating the Results We Seek
After we establish what results we are looking for, we must select the goals to get us there. Without a plan, our actions and our outcome are directionless.

Executives and managers commonly confuse end results and goals. This confusion often occurs in a complex business environment where goals compete for resources. Because success is measured by end results, a person's mind becomes fixated on *what* he wants, rather than on *how* he is going to get it. A business person may want to: (1) Be the industry leader in three years, (2) Provide a newly competitive offering in six months, (3) Train 90 percent of the sales force in one month, (4) Increase sales by 30 percent in one year, and (5) Reduce cost by 10 percent by the end of next quarter. People who want these results need to select certain goals that will lead them to produce these results (Figure 14).

After deciding on end results, the first step is to *select* (not set) the proper goals that will produce the end results. Then, we must *set* the goals to establish the degree of effort required and define the level of attainment (height of the mark) we or others must reach. Goals substantiate some measure of progress toward satisfying an opportunity or conquering a challenge. The attainment of certain goals along the way are what makes the end results possible. End results (what we want) and goals (guides to attainment) become distinguishable through Theory *I*. Different goals chart different courses. Each goal has its own attributes and respective focuses for creating success.

The source of demands for expected end results can be external or internal, such as: "My manager told me I must produce one proposal per week," or "I have decided to run a mile in under eight minutes, three times per week, to improve my general health." Whether demands for results are established by external or internal forces, we need to consider the types of goals necessary before taking any steps. The motivation, development, and performance (MDP) required for producing end results depend upon the appropriateness of the goals we select (Figure 15). Inappropriate goals can virtually destroy all of the MDP needed to produce what we want.

Figure 15

The Focus for Winning
Coach Pat Summit, the winningest coach in women's college basketball, encourages her players to focus on performance, not past mistakes. Positive reinforcement gives players confidence to face challenges and not shy away from adversaries.

Keeping goals from conflicting enhances our chances of success. It is not uncommon for external (i.e., corporate) and internal (i.e., personal) goals to conflict. Through Theory *I* we can construct parallel goals to satisfy both external and internal goals simultaneously.

As we saw earlier, focusing on what generates success is different from focusing on end results or rewards. Ideal focuses are on the attributes that create the results. Focusing solely on results produces more frustration due to the disparity between expectations and performance. Certainly feedback is necessary for telling us when we missed the mark; otherwise, making the correct adjustments would be almost impossible. The focus that leads us to making the needed adjustments must be centered on the attributes that can correct behavior for making the adjustment.

For example: Suppose you were bowling and could clearly see the pins. Just as your ball was about to hit the pins, a curtain dropped between you and the pins. You hear the crash, but you cannot see what pins remain. For you to effectively bowl your next ball, you need feedback on which pins remain (the elements), how the ball's angle of approach will direct pins to fall into other pins (the principles), and what you need to do (strategy) to use this principle to knock down each remaining pin.

Feedback is crucial to properly address the given situation. Feedback must be defined, made meaningful, and carefully employed through elements, principles, and strategies. To clarify feedback it is important to recognize there are different relationships for different goals. How these elements (identified from feedback) interact is dependent upon principles. What we do to impact positive results is determined by the strategy we use—how we swing our arm and release the ball (the attributes)—all of which determines the speed of the ball and the curvature of the ball's path.

To be effective, managers need to focus on creating an environment that fosters **synergism** (attribute) between employees to generate overall and individual effectiveness in producing an *accomplishment* (Primary Goal element). **Synergism** is the joint action of people and methodologies that, when taken together, increase each other's effectiveness. *Marketing* people focus on **selling** (attribute) to form *agreements* (Primary Goal element) with decision makers regarding the value of the features, advantages, and benefits of their products and services. Different goals, different relationships, and their respective attributes all produce different results.

An attribute of a successful bowler is **skill** in meeting specific situations of ten pins or various configurations of spares. The goal is to *achieve* the knocking down of all ten pins on the first attempt or remaining pins on the second attempt. The relationship supporting this goal is *mastery*. The desirable end result is to have the highest score based upon performance in knocking down pins. If the bowler is thinking about the high score during the approach and release of the ball, he is not focusing on the attribute of **skill**, and the results are disappointing. The bowler needs a strategy to knock down those pins and the **skill** to make it happen. The successful bowler remembers how to use his **skills** in different situations to ensure that there will not be any pins left standing. Therefore, his goal and relationship support one another because he has made the most of his attribute, **skill**. The goal of *achievement* is met through a relationship of *mastery*.

The Need for the Five Primary Goals

The surest way to frustration and failure is to indiscriminately expect positive results from everything we pursue. We need to make conscious choices in our goals. Imagine if we could look back on the lives of famous and *accomplished* people before the point in their lives when they *achieved* their successes.

A story about a girl born in Washington County, New York in 1860, tells of a mother who insisted her oldest child work to support the family. In her early teens this child began to paint, but her mother told her to put down the paint brushes and pick up a scrub brush to wash floors in neighboring homes. They needed the money for raising her nine younger brothers and sisters. The girl pleaded with her mother to no avail. Her mother chose a goal of *accomplishment* for her (scrubbing floors) when the girl wanted to choose a goal of *achievement* (art).

This dutiful young girl finally left home, married a man named Thomas Moses, and raised ten children of her own. Her painting remained a distant dream until after her children had left home. With arthritis, failing eye sight, and no painting lessons, at the age of 76 Grandma Moses began to paint. Whether we choose the wrong goal through ignorance or influence, the result can be years of missed opportunities, confusion, and frustration.

Introducing the First Classification of Elements— The Primary Goals

1. *Accomplishment* through **Maximizing Effectiveness**

Accomplishment is a goal that requires **maximizing effectiveness** of a repeat performance. When we have done something before and need to do it again, it is an *accomplishment*. This element is the opposite of *achievement*, which is to do something successfully for the first time. The attribute (**maximizing effectiveness**) focuses us on most effectively getting something *accomplished*.

Example: The first day we go to work and find our office, that is an *achievement*. The second day we go to work at our office, that is an *accomplishment*. *Accomplishments* are based upon known abilities for performances. *Achievements* are based upon development.

2. *Agreement* through **Unifying Opinions**

Agreement is a goal that requires the formation of an opinion that is in concert with the "right" thing to do, how something needs to be done, or the best product or service. When our mind-set is in synch with what is desired, no change is necessary. Since all elements are mutually exclusive, they can work completely independently, or they can support each other. One does not require the other. The attribute (**unifying opinions**) focuses us on bringing different viewpoints into *agreement*.

Example: We may *agree* with the way something needs to be

accomplished; however, we may not get it *accomplished*. We may not *agree* with the way something will be *accomplished*; however, we can still get it *accomplished*. Clearly, we do not need *agreement* to complete an *accomplishment*, or vice versa.

3. *Affiliation* through **Forming Bonds**

Affiliation is a goal that requires people to come into closer association with each other by focusing on **forming bonds.** When people are *affiliated* with each other, their support is stronger, and their attitudes and demeanors are more positive. The attribute (**forming bonds**) focuses us on creating a trust and closeness that results in *affiliation*.

The formation of bonds between people is the merging of efforts or interests for a common prerogative. These bonds can result in a close community, a supportive relationship, or a lifelong partnership (Figure 16). Each person influences the bond with the trust and acceptance of the other person. This is done through mutual respect, openness, and trust.[1]

Figure 16

The Bond of Affiliation
Affiliation is a bond that perseveres in adversity and prosperity. Without affiliation, we become weary and weakened while facing many of life's challenges.

---

1. Allan A. Cohen and David L. Bradford, *Influence Without Authority* (New York: John Wiley & Sons, 1990), 23-24.

Example: People estranged from their fellow employees or loved ones find it difficult to have positive feelings and thinking when questions arise. Negative impressions about other people can destroy *affiliation*, as well as the possibility of future quality, productive work. Strong, positive *affiliation* between individuals can eliminate unwarranted negative feelings and thinking.

4. *Affirmation* through **Confirming Wholeness**

Affirmation is a goal that **confirms wholeness** by encouraging and providing earnest assurance of a person's capabilities. When people sense equality in stature, they begin to see possibilities for their own success. The attribute (**confirming wholeness**) focuses us on building inner strength and self-worth to generate *affirmation*.

Example: People who are down and out see little hope for themselves and perhaps other people. Their negative thoughts feed upon themselves. To reverse negative personal feelings and thinking and begin making progress, a person needs to be *affirmed* as someone who can make a difference in his own life as well as in others.

5. *Achievement* through **Ensuring Growth**

Achievement is a goal of development that takes people beyond their past performances. The attribute (**ensuring growth**) focuses us on stretching our abilities to produce an *achievement*.

Example: To achieve a necessary level of growth, we have to adjust our expectations so that we may perform with a legitimate likelihood of success. We must seek advice, listen to feedback on our past performances, consider new directions, and make adjustments.

The Primary Goals form a continuum within the Table of Success Elements. *Accomplishments* are centered on pure performance, and *achievements* are centered on pure development. *Agreements* seek certain performances while recognizing that some development of opinions will be necessary. *Affiliation* with another person allows for equal performance and development on both sides. *Affirmation* often is needed for people whose performance is considerably low with a strong need for development. *Achievement* represents a pure need for development.

Procedures for Using The Table of Success Elements

For each class of elements, it is suggested that you begin at the top left side and progress to the right, indicating "yes" and "no" responses for each key element question. Take note of any "no" responses because they are the key elements we must focus on. Then progress to the next classification, moving down the table. Each "no" response will require a strategy based upon the key elements from each class. After going through the Table of Success Elements, it will be necessary to decide in which order the strategies will be fulfilled, to avoid conflict and increase chances of success. This becomes your superstrategy. The process of creating strategies will be discussed in chapter 7.

Suppose we picked an end result of increasing corporate profits by 30 percent over a two-year period. One strategy may be to develop a new product. Another strategy may be to train the sales force. If we train the sales force before developing the new product, the training effort would be wasted, and the subsequent product launch would likely fail. Therefore, our superstrategy should sequence the development of the new product first and the creation of training programs second.

Primary Goals, Attributes, and Key Element Questions
G1 - *Accomplishment* - Maximizing Effectiveness

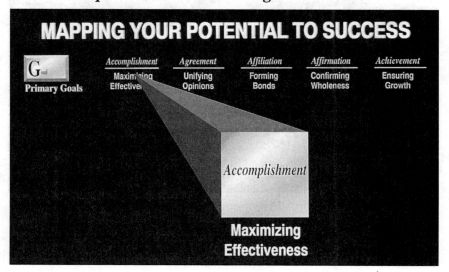

Key element question: "Are all routine tasks performed at the expected/required level of proficiency?" Since an *accomplishment* is the act of carrying out tasks by people who are accustomed to doing them, no surprises are expected with regard to these people's abilities. *Accomplishment*, in the purest sense of the word, is 100 percent dependent upon known tasks and prior encounters for performance.

> To personalize this key element question we might ask, "Am I performing all routine tasks at the required level of proficiency?" or "Is my employee performing all routine tasks at the required level of proficiency?" or "Is my client asking the usual questions about my services that he needs to ask in order to make a wise decision?"

G2 - *Agreement* - Unifying Opinions

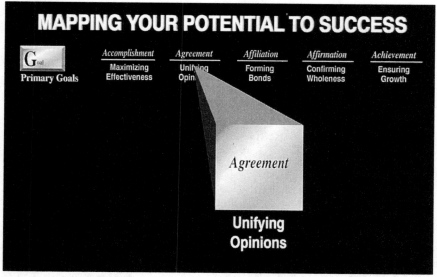

Key element question: "Are people concurring on what and how things need to be done?" *Agreement* is a coming together of opinions between two or more people regarding all terms and conditions.

We may *agree* to work toward a particular goal for a particular compensation. The process of gaining *agreement* is based mostly upon performance and end results, and to some degree on development of new ideas.

> To personalize this key element question we might ask, "Am I in concurrence with others on what and how things need to be done?" or "Does my employee concur with me on what and how things need to be done?" or "Does my client concur with the value of the service my company is offering?"

To change a person's mind we must seek common ground from which new ideas are expressed. This will add another dimension to the person's opinion and maintain that person's vested interest in a joint course of action. We need to maintain confidence through understanding. *"Selling, buying, negotiating are so much smoother and easier when the parties enjoy each other's confidence."*
—John J. McGuirk

G3 - *Affiliation* - Forming Bonds

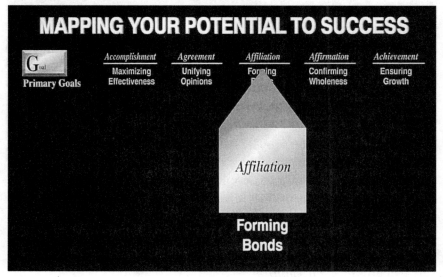

Key element question: "Are people working closely together while supporting the overall efforts?" *Affiliation* is a close association between people that ranges from friendship to the closest bonds. *Affiliation* is a uniting in fellowship that increases development and meaningfulness through **sharing**. When a relationship stops growing, *affiliation* begins to disintegrate.

To personalize this key element question we might ask, "Can I work well with other people while supporting both of our efforts?" or "Can my employee work well with other people while supporting the efforts of others?" or "Are my spouse and I **sharing** time and decisions that will bring us closer together?

G4 - *Affirmation* - Confirming Wholeness

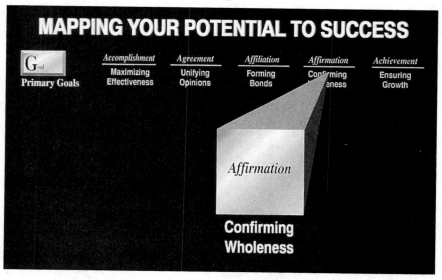

Key element question: "Are people supported in easing burdens and meeting personal needs?" *Affirmation* is the establishment of a strong and positive self. When a person's need for development overshadows his ability to perform, some form of *affirmation* becomes necessary before progress is made. People who have low self-esteem need *affirmation*.

To personalize this key element question we may ask, "Am I aware of and sensitive to personal needs and burdens of other people?" or "Is my employee aware of and sensitive to personal needs and burdens of other people?" or "Are people gaining self-respect and self-confidence when they are supported by assistance programs?"

Affirmation ensures people think well enough of themselves to feel capable of overcoming present difficulties. *Affirmation* seeks the possibilities of success in difficult situations. *"I've never met a person, I don't care what his condition, in whom I could not see possibilities. I don't care how much a man may consider himself a failure, I believe in him, for he can change the thing that is wrong in his life anytime he is prepared and ready to do it. Whenever he develops the desire, he can take away from his life the thing that is defeating it. The capacity for reformation and change lies within."* —Preston Bradley

G5 - *Achievement* - Ensuring Growth

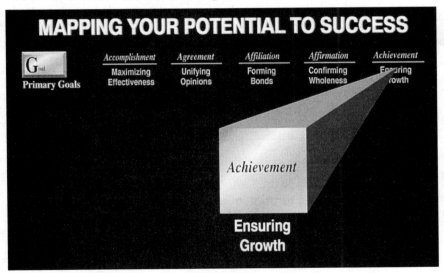

Key element question: "Are people developing new abilities to do what they need to do?" An *achievement* is the act of producing

results for the first time. *Achievement* is the purest result of development. *Achievement* requires growth.

> To personalize this key element question we may ask, "Am I perfecting and developing what I need to do to meet corporate and personal objectives?" or "Is my employee perfecting and developing what he needs to do?" "Is our business developing to increase opportunities for all people?"

A goal of *achievement* opens all possibilities for us. *"To be what we are, and to become what we are capable of becoming, is the only end of life."* —Spinoza

---

MAPPING YOUR POTENTIAL TO SUCCESS
THE TABLE OF SUCCESS ELEMENTS
WITH KEY ELEMENT QUESTIONS
("No" responses indicate key elements.)

↓ Increasing Participation ← Performance...........................Balance...........................Developme▮

Goal	*Accomplishment* Maximizing Effectiveness G1	*Agreement* Unifying Opinions G2	*Affiliation* Forming Bonds G3	*Affirmation* Confirming Wholeness G4	*Achievemer* Ensuring Growth G5
Primary Goals [Equivalent Sets w/R]	Are all routine tasks performed at the expected/ required level of proficiency?	Are people concurring on what and how things need to be done?	Are people working closely together while supporting the overall efforts?	Are people supported in easing burdens and meeting personal needs?	Are people developing n▮ abilities to d▮ what they ne▮ to do?

Goals should be guides to fulfilling our potential or what is possible within the context of our influence. The goals we reach become a concrete realization of our potential. To begin the process of aligning our potential with our performance, we need to go the next step and attach a relationship to each goal.

If we expect *agreement* when our Primary Goal is actually one of *accomplishment*, we may destroy the simplest and most practical path to the result we seek. Different relationships, such as *manage-*

ment or *marketing*, support different goals. The effectiveness of our strategies is increased when goals and relationships are properly paired.

Basic Relationships, Attributes, and Key Element Questions

Why should people be concerned about correlating goals with relationships? Nothing happens related to a goal until a Basic Relationship is attached to it. That relationship may be learning how to complete a task (*mastery*), or it could be getting someone who already knows how to complete that task to do it for us (*management*).

The connection between Primary Goals and Basic Relationships in set theory is an *equivalent set*. This means that for each goal there is a specific relationship and no other. The equivalent sets are vertically connected. For example, a goal of *accomplishment* is the result of a *management* relationship. *Agreement* is NOT the result of *management*. *Agreement* is the successful result of a *marketing* relationship. For a diagram of the equivalent sets in Theory *I*, please see the Primary Goal and Basic Relationship classifications in appendix B.

Figure 17

***Managing* for Accomplishment**
We must **maximize effectiveness** of individuals to ensure they are ready to contribute their best. A team is strengthened when its players are performing up to their potential.

R1 - *Management* - Synergism

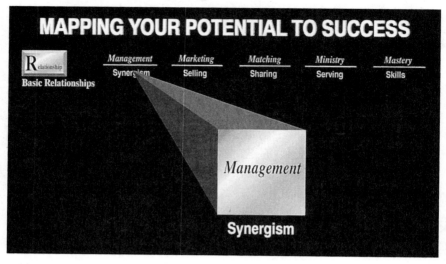

MAPPING YOUR POTENTIAL TO SUCCESS

| R elationship | Management | Marketing | Matching | Ministry | Mastery |
| Basic Relationships | Synergism | Selling | Sharing | Serving | Skills |

Management

Synergism

<u>Key element question</u>: "Is it impossible for people to enhance their performances by joint efforts?"

Managers are interested in certain, simple facts: Was the job *accomplished* on time at a reasonable cost and at a satisfactory level of performance? How the job is completed is of less interest than the fact that it was completed. When a person cannot do something by themselves, *management* can either give the person the opportunity to learn (*master*) the **skills**, or it can employ other people who have already *mastered* the **skills** to aid the person by *accomplishing* the task for them. We are now ready to begin the task of going through the GRIDS to solve a problem. There are five parts to the following example.

To illustrate use of this key element question we may consider: "The Work Place" (Part 1): A manager says, "My employees are not cooperating with me." Is this a problem or the symptom of a problem? Because false impressions may have shaped this opinion, we need to use GRIDS to probe deeper, to locate the real problem. We begin by asking the first Primary Goal key element question [G1], "Are all routine tasks performed at the expected/required level of proficiency?" We continue across the Goals Classification row until all five key element questions are answered. Next, we prioritize to select the most pressing of the key elements. In this case we will assume the "no" answer to the key element question in G1 was the biggest concern. Therefore, *management* [R1] must be brought into the relationship to begin to build a strategy. The next key element question must then come from the Basic Relationship *management* cell [R1]: "Is it impossible for people to enhance their performances by joint efforts?" This question must also be answered "yes" or "no." If the answer is "no," we need to focus on increasing the effects of R1's attribute, **synergism**. To most effectively produce **synergism**, we will have to use the next lower level of GRIDS, which will be explored in Chapter 4. When the manager said, "My employees are not cooperating with me," he may have inappropriately identified a symptom as the problem. If the manager had then counselled the employee regarding an "uncooperative" attitude, their bond of affiliation would likely have suffered because of miscommunication. If the real problem had been *accomplishment*, and an employee knew there was a better way of *accomplishing* the work through the use of another person or method, their apparent "lack of cooperation" could be eliminated through an effective *management* decision that brings about **synergism**. After **synergism** is established as a need, the *manager* may conclude that another employee, who has that **skill**, could assist. Or the *manager* may conclude a computer program could *accomplish* the job much faster.

Coordinating the resources and **skills** of other people is often better than attempting to *accomplish* a task alone (Figure 17). *"The man who gets the most satisfactory results is not always the man with the most brilliant single mind, but rather the man who can best coordinate the brains and talents of his associates."* —W. Alton Jones

The attribute of **synergism** focuses on combining unique contributions from each individual. This adds value to the overall mix of quality and productivity of the group. The purpose of focusing on **synergism** is to be certain that all avenues of getting the job done through *accomplishment* are investigated. *Management* is in an equivalent set arrangement with *accomplishment*.

Figure 18

Marketing* for *Agreement
Forming lasting *agreements* is contingent on **unifying opinions**. When our expectations coincide, there is no room for disappointment. Making a realistic assessment of a situation is critical to establishing appropriate goals and anticipating end results.

R2 - *Marketing* - Selling

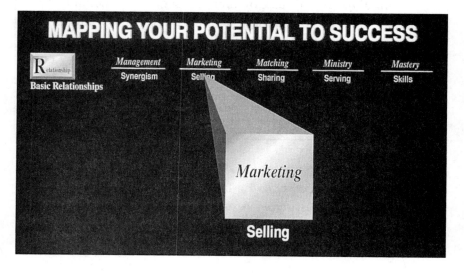

<u>Key element question</u>: "Are discussions or suggestions satisfying needs and desires of individuals?" **Selling** occurs when features of a product, service, or idea offer personal and corporate benefits at a reasonable expenditure of time and money. By satisfying the needs and desires of all parties involved, people become willing to invest. Changing minds requires forming an *agreement* through the activity of *marketing*.

To illustrate use of this key element question we may consider: "The Work Place" (Part 2): Suppose the key element question in G2 raised the biggest concern. Perhaps the *manager* needs to establish a relationship of *marketing* with those employees who disagree by asking, "Are discussions or suggestions satisfying needs and desires of individuals?" (There are unlimited ways the user may make the key element questions more specific, per the case involved.) In this instance, the manager would likely build on the original key element question [G2] by asking, "How do you think this job should be done?" This *marketing* relationship will uncover the grounds for disagreement, eliminating consideration of any so-called "uncooperative nature" of the employees. Managers sometimes need to allow employees opportunities to teach the managers something. Suppose a marketing person says, "Customers do not appreciate the selling efforts we make to ensure they buy our products and services." Again, this is a symptom, not a problem. The avenue for establishing the right goal is uncovered by asking the Primary Goal key element question for agreement [G2], "Are people concurring on what and how things need to be done?" If the answer is "no," we need to set aside the element of *agreement* and enter into a Basic Relationship of *marketing*. This is done by asking the Basic Relationship key element question for *marketing* [R2], "Are discussions or suggestions satisfying needs and desires of individuals?" If the answer is "no," then we need to focus on **selling**. As introduced in Part 1, eventually we will consider all of the remaining classifications following Goals and Relationships to resolve the concern.

One purpose of **selling** is to eliminate the difference between the expectations (features, advantages, benefits, etc.) of the buyer and of the seller (Figure 18). In the process of gaining a*greement, "Two things, well considered, would prevent many quarrels: first, to have it well ascertained whether we are not disputing about terms rather than things and, second, to examine whether that on which we differ is worth contending about."* —Colton

Unifying opinions (the attribute for *agreement*) requires a relationship of *marketing* and an attribute of **selling**. *Marketing* is in an equivalent set arrangement with *agreement*.

Figure 19

Matching* for *Affiliation People **form bonds** when they spend time together, whether it be working or relaxing. When we make up for others' shortcomings, we strengthen our effectiveness together.

R3 - *Matching* **- Sharing**

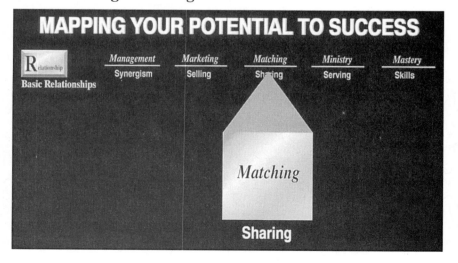

<u>Key element question</u>: "Do people's strengths balance and complement each other?" Opposites do attract, and the matching of strengths and weaknesses can form enduring bonds; however, our purpose is not dependency, but rather fulfillment. People can become fulfilled when they are able to be around and learn from those who have strengths where they are weakest. *"We gain nothing by being with such as ourselves; we encourage each other in mediocrity. I am always longing to be with men more excellent than myself."* —Lamb

To illustrate use of this key element question we may consider: "The Work Place" (Part 3): Suppose the key element question in G3 raised the biggest concern. Relating to the complaint, "My employees are not cooperating with me," perhaps the employees did not sense any *affiliation* with other members of the group, with their manager, or with their company. *Affiliation* would then become the key element that would enter into an equivalent set relationship with *matching*. If *affiliation* becomes a goal, the key element question for the manager then becomes, "Do my employees' strengths balance and complement each other?" If the answer is "no," then we need to focus on **sharing** to fix the matter. When bonds between people become closer, they tend to forgive and understand differences, even in the most difficult times. Rather than exacting points for the sake of argument, they provide the necessary support to meet the challenge. When the Primary Goal key element question for *affiliation* [G3], "Are people working closely together while supporting the overall efforts?" is answered "no," then we need to ask the Basic Relationship key element question for *matching* [R3], "Do people's strengths balance and complement each other?" More specifically, a manager may ask, "Are my employees working closely together while supporting the overall efforts?" If the answer is "no," then we need an element of *affiliation* to guide us while focusing on **forming bonds**. Then, as before, we would use the above procedure to attach a relationship to address that concern.

A healthy *affiliation* is one of honor, respect, and appreciation, rather than jealousy, control and subservience, or growing dependency. In a fifty-fifty relationship, a **sharing** of ourselves is facilitated (Figure 19). Some people sense a personal loss in relationships where $1 + 1 = 1.5$: one person is restricted in what they can offer to the relationship. When people fight over who has the greatest dominance within the relationship, chances are they are ignoring the benefit of mutually satisfying key weaknesses. We will use the entire GRIDS matrix to incorporate elements for exploring the potential within our relationships so that $1 + 1 = \infty$. *Matching* is in an equivalent set arrangement with *affiliation*.

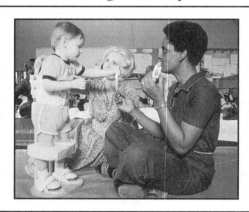

Figure 20

Ministry for *Affirmation*
Whether or not there is *accomplishment, agreement,* or even *affiliation,* the goal here is *affirmation*:
to **confirm wholeness** in a *ministry* relationship of **service**.

R4 - *Ministry* - Serving

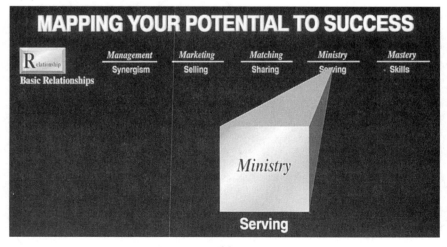

MAPPING YOUR POTENTIAL TO SUCCESS

Relationship Basic Relationships	Management Synergism	Marketing Selling	Matching Sharing	Ministry Serving	Mastery Skills

Ministry

Serving

<u>Key element question</u>: "Do people lend support to other people needing self-assurance and direction?" *Ministry* is the helping of another person without any expectation of benefit or favor in return. We openly help people because we relate to them as fellow human beings. Not because of similar beliefs, not because they will appreciate what we do, not that they will even initially agree with us or our help, not that they will love us in return, but because they will be better for it (Figure 20). The attribute of **serving** focuses on supporting another person without the expectation of a direct or indirect reward.

We, too, benefit from *ministry*, whether or not that is our intention. *"We cannot hold a torch to light another's path without brightening our own."* —Ben Sweetland. Our intentions in *ministry* must be genuine for the results to truly fulfill our goals. *"If things are not going well with you, begin your effort at correcting the situation by carefully examining the service you are rendering, and especially the spirit in which you are rendering it."* —Roger Babson. *Ministry* is in an equivalent set arrangement with *affirmation*.

To illustrate use of this key element question we may consider: "The Work Place" (Part 4): Suppose the key element question in G4 raised the biggest concern. The manager may still assume employees lack cooperation. However, the employees' lack of confidence in doing anything right in the eyes of the boss may be the culprit. Afraid of making mistakes, the employees procrastinate until the last minute, when they must rush. This creates needless errors and stress along the way.

Suppose you have employees who are depressed and ready to give up for a variety of personal or professional reasons. Since the response to the Primary Goal key element question for *affirmation* [G4], "Are people supported in easing burdens and meeting personal needs?" is "no," we need to establish a Primary Goal of *affirmation*, focus on **confirming wholeness**, and form the equivalent set relationship of *ministry*. The Basic Relationship key element question for *ministry* [R4] is, "Do people lend support to other employees needing self-assurance and direction?" If the answer is "no," then we need to focus on **serving**.

Figure 21
***Mastering* for
*Achievement***
By focusing on **ensuring
growth**, we reduce the fear
of failure and begin the
skill building process.

R5 - *Mastery* - Skills

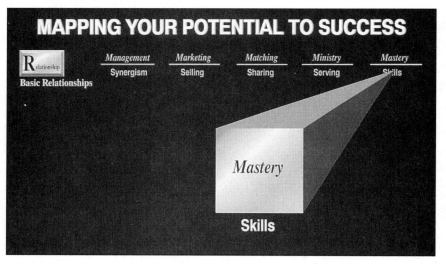

Key element question: "Are people consistently developing their expertise for effectiveness?"

Mastery is the development of new abilities to expand our opportunities and to reach potential. The focus in *mastery* is on development of **skills** of the worker, thereby avoiding undue dependence on others. In *mastery*, we attribute our success to our new **skills**. **Skill** development contrasts with the opposite end of the classification: **synergism**, which is the application of previously established **skills**.

To illustrate use of this key element question we may consider: "The Work Place" (Part 5): Suppose the key element question in G5 raised the biggest concern. The manager should recognize that the employees' lack of cooperation may be caused by their confusion or sense of inadequacy. The necessary goal of *achievement* can be met by focusing on **ensuring growth**.

Suppose an individual is not doing well in his work. The manager needs to ask a question that builds on the Primary Goal key element question for *achievement* [G5] of "Are people developing new abilities to do what they need to do?" He further asks, "Are the employees developing new abilities to do what they have been assigned to do?" If the answer is "no," then he needs the goal of *achievement* to enter into an equivalent set relationship with *mastery*. If the answer to the Basic Relationship key element question for *mastery* [R5], "Are people consistently developing their expertise for effectiveness?" is "no," then their needs to be a focus on developing **skills**.

We form a Basic Relationship of *mastery* by bridging our old self (emotions and logic) and our new self to develop **skills** to our fullest personal potential (Figure 21). Change can be healthy, especially if we know the variables at work and the formula that makes everything work out. *"Undertake something that is difficult; it will do you good. Unless you try to do something beyond what you have already mastered, you will never grow."* —Ronald E. Osborn. The attribute of **skill** focuses individuals on developing new capabilities or reviving old capabilities to increase their personal assets. *Mastery* is in an equivalent set arrangement with *achievement*.

MAPPING YOUR POTENTIAL TO SUCCESS
THE TABLE OF SUCCESS ELEMENTS
WITH KEY ELEMENT QUESTIONS
("No" responses indicate key elements.)

↓Increasing Participation ← Performance............................Balance............................Development→

Goal **Primary Goals** [Equivalent Sets w/R]	*Accomplishment* **Maximizing Effectiveness** G1 Are all routine tasks performed at the expected/ required level of proficiency?	*Agreement* **Unifying Opinions** G2 Are people concurring on what and how things need to be done?	*Affiliation* **Forming Bonds** G3 Are people working closely together while supporting the overall efforts?	*Affirmation* **Confirming Wholeness** G4 Are people supported in easing burdens and meeting personal needs?	*Achievement* **Ensuring Growth** G5 Are people developing new abilities to do what they need to do?
Relationship **Basic Relationships** [Equivalent Sets w/G]	*Management* **Synergism** R1 Is it impossible for people to enhance their performances by joint efforts?	*Marketing* **Selling** R2 Are discussions or suggestions satisfying needs and desires of individuals?	*Matching* **Sharing** R3 Do people's strengths balance and complement each other?	*Ministry* **Serving** R4 Do people lend support to other people needing self-assurance and direction?	*Mastery* **Skills** R5 Are people consistently developing their expertise for effectiveness?

In this chapter, we have discovered the connection of goals that lead us to an end result, and the relationships that can support us in reaching those goals. We are now prepared to examine the various choices of ideologies (assumptions in each of our relationships with other people) that we can use to fulfill relationships and satisfy those goals.

Chapter 4

THE PRINCIPAL IDEOLOGIES
OF COMMUNICATION

We analyze sources of communication problems and adjust our actions accordingly to satisfy opportunities by addressing: **How We See Other People**; **Principal Ideologies, Attributes, and Key Element Questions**; **Creating Subsets for Principal Ideologies**; and **The Five Principal Ideologies in Summary**.

How We See Other People

How we see other people is influenced by who we are, as well as who they are. This is because we see people through the filters of our experiences, rather than simply as they are. We depend on our own insights (gained through experiences), which may lead us to overemphasize or underestimate some aspects of the person. We also make assumptions about what we need to do to get certain people to work effectively. Assumptions are at the center of how we interact, build trust, gain cooperation, and lead people to success or failure.

Five principal assumptions about people guide us in our interaction with them. Three of these principal assumptions about people have been well documented over the years and have become standard terms in management practices and literature. These recognized bodies of doctrine were founded on inaccurate perceptions and impractical theorizing. These incomplete ideologies are referred to as Theories X, Y, and Z. A fourth ideology attempts to make up for the inadequacies of the three by combining them: Theory M. A fifth ideology, Theory *I*, upgrades the other ideologies to make them practical and effective when addressing particular situations. We will explore all five ideologies and how each of the first four becomes a *subset* of the fifth. For a diagram of the subsets in Theory *I*, please see the Principal Ideology classification in appendix B.

Principal Ideologies, Attributes, and Key Element Questions

Ideologies are a means of influencing other people to do something. Within the Principal Ideology classifications of elements there are five choices for tailoring our assumptions to increase effectiveness, cooperation, team efforts, and all other means for communicating.

I1 - Theory *X* - Command

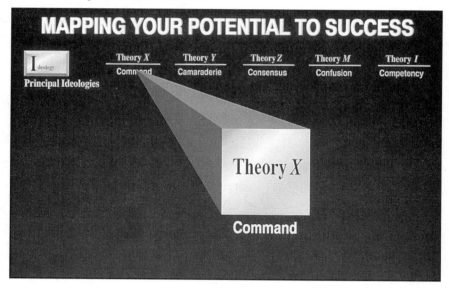

Theory *X*: *"A Theory X manager assumes that people are fundamentally lazy, irresponsible, and need to be constantly watched."* —Douglas M. McGregor, MIT professor

Key element question: "Do people know what to do and how to do it without being told to perform?"

The answer to this question would be, "No," if the leader were a pharaoh who needed thousands of workers some 4,500 years ago to build a pyramid. These massive structures covered the equivalent of 10 football fields. To manage such a large undertaking, the pharaoh needed total control and authority over people to satisfy his wishes. Work was difficult and even life threatening, but the pharaoh and those whom he designated as his first-line managers were forceful enough to ensure the work was accomplished.

In a point of view explained by Douglas McGregor, Theory X showed little respect for people as individuals. McGregor's Theory X asserted that people were not dependable.[1] The greater the power given a manager, the greater became the manager's propensity to become Theory X. As employees became more educated, Theory X became less warranted and tolerated.

A new workplace, with static personnel and production needs, was created as a result of new production processes. In 1798, Eli Whitney was approached by the U.S. government to produce 10,000 muskets in two years. Whitney went to Washington in 1800 with 500 muskets. In response to questions about missing the deadline, Whitney placed piles of identical musket parts on tables and asked these government officials to bring him a piece from each pile. To their amazement, he put together a musket that worked! Whitney had invented the standardization of parts. This meant that masses of trained workers, rather than highly skilled musket specialists, could make the 10,000 muskets. The only variable to address would be hiring and paying enough people to get the job done.

With the idea of mass production growing in popularity, Henry Ford applied the concept to assembly lines for the manufacturing of automobiles in the early 1900s. Due to the mundane nature of assembly line work, it became necessary for Ford to increase the average hourly wage fivefold to attract line workers. Workers began sacrificing self-fulfillment for better salaries. They became "motivated"

1. Douglas D. McGregor, *The Human Side of Enterprise*, 25th Anniversary Printing ed. (New York: McGraw-Hill, 1985), 33-34.

by money, and this made them subject themselves to a management solely interested in that pursuit. They became psychologically controlled by money. Theory X managers focus on their own power and knowledge by believing, "We know exactly how everything should be, must be, and ought to be done. All employees know nothing until they are told what to do."

Eventually, work at the Ford plant became more and more unbearable. Management began viewing its role as an enforcer of quality and quantity levels. The "We vs. They" management relationship (Theory X) resurfaced in the industrial age. The more frustrated American managers became, the more they intensified their efforts to get results out of their workers. Unions were formed in response to Theory X managers forcing people to work in unfit environments. Managers insisted on their set levels of production first; workers focused on trying to get salary increases in exchange for meeting those levels. Personal fulfillment at work was something no one pursued.

There are advantages to strong leadership and influences afforded to employees working under Theory X. However, these advantages can be assured only when combined as a subset of Theory I and denoted as Theory I_X.

The workplace changed over the years. People became educated and performed specialized work; they were known as *knowledge workers*. These workers did not respond to the tenets of Theory X in the same manner as laborers, and a whole new approach to management developed. Knowledge workers could not be threatened as easily or monitored as closely as production workers. The real value of knowledge workers would be reduced through an insulting relationship of Theory X. The requirement for the creation of a new management ideology was defined by McGregor as Theory Y and was seen as the way of the future.

I2 - Theory *Y* - Camaraderie

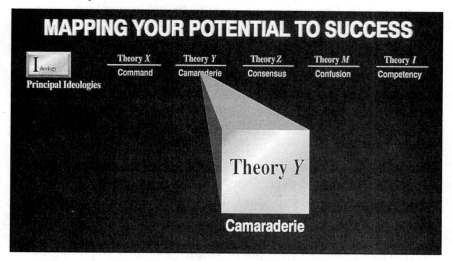

Theory *Y*: *"A Theory Y manager assumes that people are funda-mentally hard-working, responsible, and need only to be supported and encouraged."* —Douglas M. McGregor

<u>Key element question</u>: "Do people have the freedom to do what is most meaningful and gratifying?" The answer is, "Yes," when knowledge is the center of judgment and decision making. Theory *Y* works when people make choices that support themselves as well as the organization. They are more productive and happier.

This management philosophy worked as long as individuals could clearly see their role and contribute through self-directed efforts; however, as the complexity of organizations grew in size, creating more sophisticated products and services, the knowledge worker became more self-**serving** (*ministering* to their own needs), and less interested in promoting the goals of the organization. Employees became more concerned with details of the dental plan, retirement programs, and promotions than they were about the mission of the organization or any particular value of their contribution.

For instance, one award-winning Fortune 500 company had a flawed, top secret, worldwide functional corporate strategy. The first problem with this strategy was that access to this document was restricted. The functional strategy would never be known by those who could ensure it was implemented. The second problem was that the thick document contained so much corporate dogma on success that no one would have the interest or time to study it. The third and most glaring problem was that, in this inch and a half thick document designed to focus a worldwide organization, the word "customer" did not appear once! Several years later, this company decided to announce a special program entitled, "The Year of the Customer."

This organization had used Theory *Y* successfully; its people were discovering, developing, and reporting critical information. However, the management team negated the positive effects of this Theory *Y* freedom when they vacillated between irresponsible, carefree management (allowing run-away expenses) and over control (numerous restrictions, detailed reporting, and needs for approval for minor decisions). Management even ignored suggestions submitted by their own employees in feedback programs. Ultimately, the managers' barriers dissuaded the employees from speaking out or suggesting new ideas.

Another example in this same organization epitomizes the Theory *Y* management ideology. For six months a particular employee worked for his boss. He had never been called in to discuss work in progress or asked to attend a meeting. One morning, the manager approached the employee and said, "I need to see you sometime in my office before noon today! Please see Rita, my secretary, to schedule some time with me this morning." The tone of voice indicated that something important was about to transpire.

Later, at the meeting, the manager smiled, leaned forward, and whispered, "Today is Rita's birthday. We have bought her a cake. I wanted you to sign the birthday card. I will need you here by my office at noon, so we can all surprise her and sing 'Happy Birthday.'" Real missions or objectives were seldom discussed in this organization. Exaggerated significance was placed on events (like birthdays), which were faithfully covered with special occasion cards, cakes, and celebrations.

Current views on Theory X and Theory Y state that internal and external factors influence the approach to management. However, there is little indication as to which approach should be used. Instead of a focus on either the structure or the human side of organizations, there has been an emphasis on the integration of these two things, as well as consideration of environmental and other external influences.[2]

Even though managers may have many styles, Theories X and Y have received the greatest attention. Some business thinkers believe that Theory X is appropriate when subordinates truly require external motivation. Others believe that Theory Y requires a diagnosis of the situation to help the manager choose from a repertoire of available styles. However, no effective method had been established to prescribe a solution to any problem presented.

In the Theory I methodology we can effect a solution by combining management ideologies. Later in this chapter we will discuss how to create subsets of the management ideologies to utilize only their positive qualities while discarding any negative impact.

Tom Peters and Bob Waterman claim that McGregor's theories and those related, in what is referred to as the "human relations" school of management, have been challenged. The consensus of the human relations movement as a failure was foretold by the failure to balance the excesses of the rational model. The rational model is described as a management process that addresses decision-making while ignoring "pathfinding" (the intuitive process needed in discovering better products, services, and processes) and implementation of a course of action.[3]

2. Judith A. Gordon, *Organizational Behavior*, 5th ed. (Upper Saddle River: Prentice-Hall, 1996), 11, 317, 318.

3. Thomas J. Peters and Robert H. Waterman Jr., *In Search of Excellence* (New York: Harper & Row, 1982), 52-54, 95-96.

I3 - Theory *Z* - Consensus

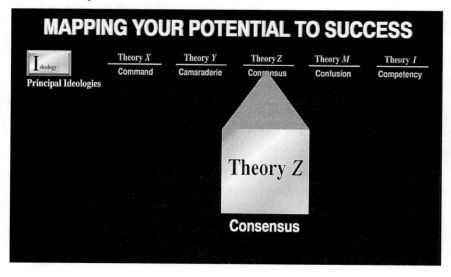

Theory *Z*: *"A Theory Z manager assumes that people thoroughly schooled in a distinct corporate culture with long-range staff development will have consensus decision-making without being watched or encouraged."* —William G. Ouchi, UCLA professor

Key element question: "Do people work cooperatively in support of one another as an effective team?" In the 1980s and early 1990s, when foreign competition was no longer deniable, Americans took a close look at a new form of management.

Theory *Z* is a management ideology where people are encouraged to work together as a team. This entails coordinating efforts for a team to get work done. This approach de-emphasizes the importance of individuals; supporting the team is the only acceptable course of action for the worker. This approach to management was ideal within a homogeneous culture (like Japan). In Japan, if an employee were to be singled out and brought up on stage to receive a plaque, that employee would feel embarrassed and humiliated. Theory *Z* thrives on motivation for the betterment of the team, not the individual.

Western cultures and practices treat rewards far differently. In the United States, an awarded employee would smile, feel good about himself, and be happy for the recognition. The American audience may be happy for the winner, or possibly envious, because they wanted to receive the award. Coveted awards have been known to destroy teamwork because workers may be jealous and not want to work with the awarded worker. Still others may increase efforts to earn the next award. Theory Z evaluation and promotion systems reward seniority over merit.[4]

In some Fortune 500 companies, workers formed alliances to help only certain people: those people who had the greatest chances for winning an award and being promoted. After the promotion, these supporters expected some form of compensation through bonuses or their own promotion. This was referred to as the "push-pull" means for advancement.

People who expect rapid advancement as a sign of success consider upward mobility a condition of employment. When it is not achieved, employment is sought elsewhere.[5] This mind-set is detrimental to both short-term and long-term company viability. Rather than focusing on work, these employees tend to focus on their résumés, and that point of view tends to weaken a company's capability to retain and utilize people for meeting business objectives.

Another problem with Theory Z is the danger of a company ballooning in size because it is more attentive to the requirements of keeping a team together, even if all members of that team are not performing up to standard. There is no impetus to cut off "dead weight" workers. The use of Theory Z makes companies unresponsive to drastic changes in economies, and more likely to fail, causing untold difficulty for all workers.[6]

---

4. Robert P. Vecchio, *Organizational Behavior*, 3d ed. (Fort Worth: The Dryden Press, Harcourt Brace College Publishers, 1995), 631.

5. Ibid.

6. Francis McInerney and Sean White, *The Total Quality Corporation* (New York: Truman Talley Books, 1995), 239-240.

I4 - Theory *M* - Confusion

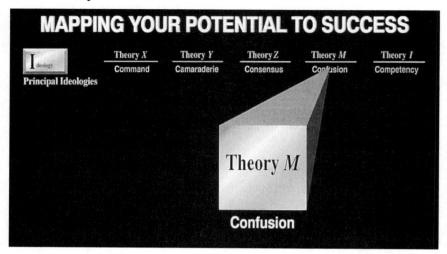

Theory *M*: *"A Theory M manager assumes that people will not adequately respond to one style of management in a consistent manner; therefore, they need to be kept off balance, defenseless, and uncertain about the future."* —Clifford I. Sears

Key element question: "When people feel job security, do they strive to increase their effectiveness?"

People who become either too subservient or too comfortable with allowing managers to make all key decisions need to become more self-reliant. By continually changing assumptions and communication styles, from Theory *X* to Theory *Y* to Theory *Z*, managers can generate enough **confusion** and frustration so that disgruntled employees empower themselves to take charge or quit. Employees begin to think, "I can do better by making my own decisions." Managers must be sure they do not discourage self-reliant behavior from those employees who effectively take charge.

The *M* in Theory *M* stands for two things: Mixed and Manipulation. The Mixed form of Theory *M* is the rotation of ideologies (Theories *X*, *Y*, and *Z*) in hopes that the individual will become more self-reliant on steady, dependable internal direction, and less dependent upon outside shifting control. Theory *M* is prevalent in teaching environments or on-the-job training. On the other hand, manipulation keeps people vulnerable and uncertain about what to expect. Managers sometimes use this latter form of Theory M in hopes that the employee will become frustrated and want to quit. This usage is prevalent in downsizing environments.

Suppose a boss charges his project team of employees with creating a product design. The boss does not tell his project team what the product should be or how to go about concluding what it should be. The project team is confused and goes to the boss, asking for more direction. They ask the boss, "Tell us, what do you expect us to do?" The boss refuses to tell them, saying he will answer any specific questions that will allow the project team to remain as the leaders of the project. But, he adds, the methods and avenues of their exploration will be left up to the project team. In frustration, the employees are forced to discover for themselves the possibilities. When they determine and evaluate their own ideas, they then can ask the boss more specific, answerable questions, such as "Does *this* product fit in with the overall corporate strategy?" The Theory M boss then gives them specific answers to provide needed guidance. He has forcibly empowered the project team to take charge (Theory X), provided the freedom to run their own project (Theory Y), and placed them in a team requiring cooperation and mutual support (Theory Z). The employees learn to rely on themselves in the face of what seems to be unpredictability and inconsistency from the manager. A Theory M manager tests the resourcefulness of his employees.

Unfortunately, in response to increasing competition and an inability to effectively use Theories X, Y, or Z, the manipulation form of Theory M has arisen. This form of Theory M has been used during downsizing to trim employees from an overpopulated work force, to intimidate other employees to work harder, or to force the remainder to quit. Theory M is ideal for destroying unhealthy attachments of subordinates to bosses, their own agenda, or the group. Through the chaos that is generated, subordinates begin to lead themselves and the organization toward prosperity.

Considering the previous example of the mixed form of Theory *M*, the manager may use the manipulation form by haphazardly alternating between styles or by not even answering specific questions from a project team. No meaningful direction or suppport would be given at all, and failure would be imminent. There would be no vent or alternative for employee frustration other than for the employee to quit.

The manipulation form of Theory *M* has pushed countless people into leaving downsizing organizations. Unfortunately for the organization, usually the most confident and capable people leave to find better work. Many of those who remain are "tree huggers" who continue to fret and waste time. This is why Theory *M* can only be used in the short term. Long-term use decreases both stability and consistency in direction. Theory *M* destroys trust and works against a cooperative spirit. Outside the training environment, Theory *M* is least likely to provide any advantage, even when combined with Theory *I*. The most common legitimate usage of Theory *M* is as an exercise to demonstrate: (1) a need for self-reliance by employees or (2) a good example of how not to manage. The notation for this Principal Ideology is Theory I_M.

I5 - Theory *I* - Competency

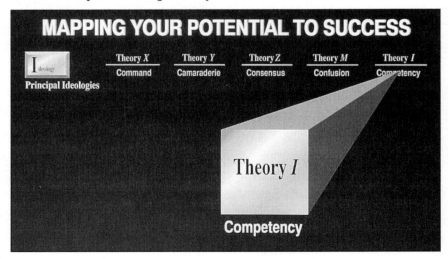

Theory *I*: *"A Theory I manager assumes that individuals schooled in how to reach personal fulfillment within declared corporate objectives need not be watched, encouraged, or manipulated into conformity or anonymity."* —Clifford I. Sears

<u>Key element question</u>: "Are people fulfilled while developing expertise to be most effective?"

Competency is demonstrated through the successful merger of capability with the completion of needed tasks (Figure 22). The more we focus on our natural talents in an effort to contribute to meeting corporate missions, the more personal fulfillment and corporate satisfaction we will produce. Though the work we do for a company belongs to that company, the skills we develop as a result of doing that work belong to us and can be used for our greater welfare. Since our potential is our greatest asset to ourselves and any organization, it behooves both to explore its possibilities by using Theory *I* and then focus on what interests us.

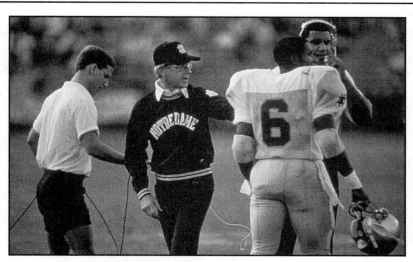

Figure 22. **Developing the Right Competencies**
Coach Lou Holtz develops the **competencies** of each player to their peak potential. When game day arrives, he knows what level of performance to expect from his players. He ensures his expectations will correlate to the actual ability of each member of the team.

In the late 1920s and early 30s, Elton Mayo of the Harvard Graduate School of Business Administration conducted many studies for the Institute for Social Research at the University of Michigan. The focus of these studies was on attitudes and behavior of first-line supervisors and how these affect the productivity of their subordinates. Mayo found that supervisors characterized as "employee centered" were likely to be in charge of high-producing groups and that those characterized as "production centered" were likely to be in charge of low-producing groups.[7] Theory *I* has been crafted to be "employee centered" and "production centered." Theory *I*, as an ideology, directs users to focus on **competency**. When this focus is met, the Theory *I* methodology can be used effectively.

Creating Subsets for Principal Ideologies

Subsets are elements contained within another element. Theories *X*, *Y*, *Z*, and *M* can function as individual subsets of Theory *I*.

Theory *X* Subset: Of the five elements that make up Principal Ideologies, suppose you knew a manager to be a Theory *X*. The standards of conduct under which this Theory *X* manager operates are: "I always demand and expect exactly what I want. I never let projects fall behind. I do not accept last-minute excuses." Employees become frightened, and productivity goes down. The solution is to create and use a subset of Theory *I*. There is nothing wrong with the standards of conduct for Theory *X* managers as long as Theory *I* is the Principal Ideology. Theory *I* always leads using the attribute of **competency**. The way we would communicate in this instance would be Theory I_X. As long as the manager can assure employee **competency** by either examination or necessary development, the establishment of high standards and the enforcement of those standards adds to the value of the employee's contribution. Of course, Principal Ideologies are only one-fifth of the GRIDS class consideration, so to complete the Theory *I* methodology for success, other classes of elements may be essential.

---

7. Saul W. Gellerman, *Motivation and Productivity* (New York: Amacom, American Management Association, 1963), 19, 32-34.

$\mathbf{I}$deology\n\n**Principal Ideologies**\n\n[Subsets of Theory I]	Theory X **Command** **I1** Theory I_X is ideal when competency precedes demand for performance.				

Theory Y Subset: Suppose you knew a manager to be a Theory Y. The standards of conduct under which this Theory Y manager operates are: "I enjoy being a manager only when everyone is happy in their working environment. I will do almost anything to avoid stress, because it works against high quality and productivity. I want everyone to feel comfortable by setting their own pace." Theory I always leads using the attribute of **competency**. The way we would communicate in this instance would be Theory I_Y. As long as the manager can assure employee **competency**, encouraging the employee through camaraderie will support productive efforts from the employee.[8] Without the assurance of **competency**, management would run the risk of appearing to reward the employee for mere friendliness.

$\mathbf{I}$deology\n\n**Principal Ideologies**\n\n[Subsets of Theory I]	Theory X **Command** **I1** Theory I_X is ideal when competency precedes demand for performance.	Theory Y **Camaraderie** **I2** Theory I_Y is ideal when competency leads freedom of performance & development.			

Theory Z Subset: Suppose you knew a manager to be a Theory Z. The standards of conduct under which this Theory Z manager operates are: "We have a team of people who must work well together in producing the best product or service. Nothing must be allowed to get

---

8. Andrew G. Goliszek, *Breaking the Stress Habit* (Winston-Salem: Carolina Press, 1987), 68.

in the way of team effectiveness. Dissenters will be punished or possibly eliminated from the team to assure harmony." The way we would communicate in this instance would be Theory I_Z. As long as the manager can assure employee **competency**, consensus is effective if directed to the benefit of the organization.

I deology Principal Ideologies [Subsets of Theory *I*]	Theory *X* Command I1 Theory I_X is ideal when competency precedes demand for performance.	Theory *Y* Camaraderie I2 Theory I_Y is ideal when competency leads freedom of performance & development.	Theory *Z* Consensus I3 Theory I_Z is ideal when competency leads formations of common approaches.		

Theory *M* Subset: Suppose you knew a manager to be a Theory *M*. The standards of conduct under which this Theory *M* manager operates are: "You need to take charge of your own job or career and maintain a positive attitude while enjoying your work. You also need to get the job done on time without making any excuses. You must be a team player and use your resources to their greatest advantage." The way we would communicate, in this instance, would be Theory I_M. As long as the manager can be sure that employees are **competent**, he may not need to provide continued supervision for work to be completed.

I deology Principal Ideologies [Subsets of Theory *I*]	Theory *X* Command I1 Theory I_X is ideal when competency precedes demand for performance.	Theory *Y* Camaraderie I2 Theory I_Y is ideal when competency leads freedom of performance & development.	Theory *Z* Consensus I3 Theory I_Z is ideal when competency leads formations of common approaches.	Theory *M* Confusion I4 Theory I_M is ideal when competency leads the road back to creating a best approach.	

Theory *I*: Suppose you knew a manager to be a Theory *I*. The standards of conduct under which this Theory *I* manager operates are: "Employees must be given the opportunity to work and grow daily to ensure they can make their greatest contributions to both the organization and themselves." The solution is to simply use Theory I. There are no "missing" concepts and no inappropriate assumptions.

Ideology **Principal Ideologies** [Subsets of Theory I]	Theory X **Command** I1 Theory I_X is ideal when competency precedes demand for performance.	Theory Y **Camaraderie** I2 Theory I_Y is ideal when competency leads freedom of performance & development.	Theory Z **Consensus** I3 Theory I_Z is ideal when competency leads formations of common approaches.	Theory M **Confusion** I4 Theory I_M is ideal when competency leads the road back to creating a best approach.	Theory I **Competency** I5 Theory I is ideal when competency leads them and everyone else to certain success.

The Five Principal Ideologies in Summary

"A Theory X manager assumes that people are fundamentally lazy, irresponsible, and need to be constantly watched." —Douglas M. McGregor.

"A Theory Y manager assumes that people are fundamentally hard-working, responsible, and need only to be supported and encouraged." —Douglas M. McGregor.

"A Theory Z manager assumes that people thoroughly schooled in a distinct corporate culture with long-range staff development will have consensus decision-making without being watched or encouraged."—William G. Ouchi

"A Theory M manager assumes that people will not adequately respond to one style of management in a consistent manner; therefore, they need to be kept off balance, defenseless, and uncertain about the future." —Clifford I. Sears

"A Theory I manager assumes that individuals schooled in how to reach personal fulfillment within declared corporate objectives need not be watched, encouraged, or manipulated into conformity or anonymity." —Clifford I. Sears

At this point we have defined an end result and selected goals to lead us to those results. We have established and built relationships that support each goal. To gain the strongest participation from people involved, we have created a set of assumptions or ideologies for producing the most positive outcome for each circumstance. Now, we are preparing to go to the deepest level of determination for commitments needed from each person.

Within the Prime Determinants we will see how this is possible through all of the elements leading up to our *individuality*. Whether we are choosing goals, relationships, ideologies, or determinants, our *individuality* must come through in order for us to control our success. In every relationship, there must be at least two strong *I*'s (competent individuals) before there can be a strong *we*. The personal implications of this process become clearly defined within the Prime Determinants classification of elements.

MAPPING YOUR POTENTIAL TO SUCCESS

THE TABLE OF SUCCESS ELEMENTS

WITH KEY ELEMENT QUESTIONS

("No" responses indicate key elements.)

ncreasing Participation ←Performance..........................Balance..........................Development →

	Accomplishment **Maximizing Effectiveness** G1	*Agreement* **Unifying Opinions** G2	*Affiliation* **Forming Bonds** G3	*Affirmation* **Confirming Wholeness** G4	*Achievement* **Ensuring Growth** G5
Goal **Primary Goals** [Equivalent Sets w/R]	Are all routine tasks performed at the expected/ required level of proficiency?	Are people concurring on what and how things need to be done?	Are people working closely together while supporting the overall efforts?	Are people supported in easing burdens and meeting personal needs?	Are people developing new abilities to do what they need to do?
	Management **Synergism** R1	*Marketing* **Selling** R2	*Matching* **Sharing** R3	*Ministry* **Serving** R4	*Mastery* **Skills** R5
Relationship **Basic Relationships** [Equivalent Sets w/G]	Is it impossible for people to enhance their performances by joint efforts?	Are discussions or suggestions satisfying needs and desires of individuals?	Do people's strengths balance and complement each other?	Do people lend support to other people needing self-assurance and direction?	Are people consistently developing their expertise for effectiveness?
	Theory *X* **Command** I1	Theory *Y* **Camaraderie** I2	Theory *Z* **Consensus** I3	Theory *M* **Confusion** I4	Theory *I* **Competency** I5
Ideology **Principal Ideologies** [Subsets of Theory *I*]	Do people know what to do and how to do it without being told to perform?	Do people have the freedom to do what is most meaningful and gratifying?	Do people work cooperatively in support of one another as an effective team?	When people feel job security, do they strive to increase their effectiveness?	Are people fulfilled while developing expertise to be most effective?

Chapter 5

THE PRIME DETERMINANTS
OF HUMAN BEHAVIOR

We understand the factors behind human behavior by addressing:
**Sources of Determination for Success; An Overview of
Prime Determinants; The Five Guidelines for Using Prime
Determinants for Personal Success;** and **Prime
Determinants, Attributes, and Key Element Questions**.

Sources of Determination for Success

"Successful people are very determined." If this is true, we need to
uncover all of the sources of determination, both internal and external
to ourselves. The best internal determinants are whatever
contributes to our good health (rest, relaxation, nourishment, and
stimulation). The best external determinants are positive support
provided by those whose opinion and direction we trust, respect,
and appreciate.

People's behavior may be determined by what other people say and
do to force them into action, such as: pay for performance through
commissions, or threats of job security, or psychological exclusion
from an inner circle of colleagues. Outside controls, like these, are
not determinations for success; rather, they are manipulations that
ultimately destroy motivation, development, and performance.

What can drain determination? People often waste their determination
on too many arguments, too many focuses, too much confusion, and
too little structure and strategy.

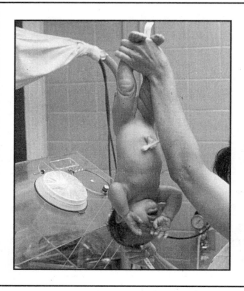

Figure 23.

How We Measure Up
Society measures all of us the best ways it knows how. But our talents and potential are immeasurable when we become conditioned to succeed. We determine for ourselves which environment will foster a cycle of success.

An Overview of Prime Determinants

Before choosing a determinant for personal efforts, a manager might ask: (1) Are employees healthy and energetic? (2) Are employees uptight, or do they naturally relax and enjoy being around each other? (3) Are employees using facts to test their beliefs? (4) Do employees have any hopes or dreams for themselves or the organization? (5) Do employees have a sense of "self" in their work?

Reactions to attributes are unique to each individual. For example, the element of *instructions* contains a set of attributes which are the **health directives** that guide our physical life. DNA, for example, determines the attributes that control the development of every animal or plant species. It is a person's attributes that determine who they are, and how successful they are (Figure 23).

In set theory, the attributes of the elements in this class represent *overlapping sets*. **Health directives** are directly impacted by our **natural tendencies**, and both of these are directly impacted by how we view **facts** and form **beliefs**. These attributes, in turn, are affected by our **hopes and dreams**, as well as our **self-determination**. For a diagram of the overlapping sets in Theory *I*, please see the Prime Determinant classification in appendix B.

The Five Prime Determinants

Instructions - our basic **health directives** determine heartbeat, involuntary breathing, blood pressure, and body temperature.

Instincts - our **natural tendencies** and social drives determine "fight or flight," parenting behavior, and drives to satisfy sex, hunger, and thirst.

Information - influences from our education and experiences determine how we interpret **facts** and form **beliefs**.

Imagination - our mind's ability to conceive **hopes** and **dreams** determines what we can envision.

Individuality - our free will or **self-determination** to shape our lives determines what we decide to do.

The Five Guidelines for Using Prime Determinants for Personal Success

Look at each key question in the Prime Determinants classification in the Table of Success Elements. Any question which can be answered "yes" should be disregarded. For the questions you have answered "no," you should consider how they need to be addressed individually and jointly with neighboring elements within the Prime Determinants classification. Because Prime Determinant elements are overlapping sets, each question's resolution will allow you to understand the emerging picture of the circumstances that created subsequent problems so that you will be able to resolve these problems as well.

The following chart provides an overview and structure for considering the elements and attributes behind the Prime Determinants and their applications. Once the determinants shown here are identified, we will be able to "decide to do whatever it takes" to produce success.

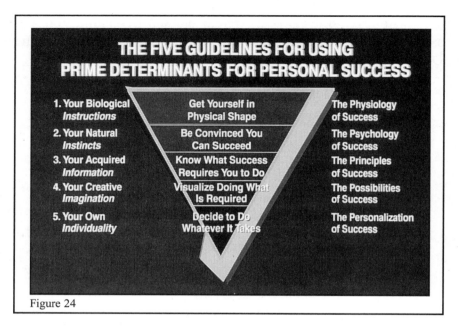

Figure 24

Prime Determinants, Attributes, and Key Element Questions

1. The Physiology of Success—Your Biological *Instructions*

D1 - *Instructions* - Health Directives

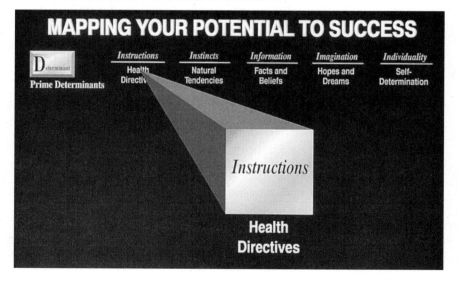

<u>Key element question</u>: "Are people physically capable and mentally alert for performing?"

Instructions are the first Prime Determinant that affect us through our motivation, development, and performance. All living organisms have *instructions*. Without these *instructions* automatically directing us as living organisms to perform all our bodily functions, we would have to figure out a way to make our heart beat, determine how to set our blood pressure, and remind ourselves to breathe! We would need a highly sophisticated graduate-level bioengineering course just to live. Exhaustion would set in, and we would have no time or energy to do anything else. Ultimately we would become tired, fall asleep, forget to generate the necessary *instructions*, and die!

Instructions are affected by our diets (Figure 25), sleep patterns, biorhythms, allergies, etc. We can appear lazy (lacking motivation) when our allergies are acting up, when we do not get enough restful sleep, or when our diet does not supply us with enough energy. We may appear ignorant (lack of performance) when, in fact, our eyeglasses need a change in prescription. We may appear unfriendly (lack of motivation and performance) when we do not hear and

Figure 25

"Care and Feeding" for Your Success
Ignoring directives (such as consuming excessive amounts of salt) may appeal to short-term contentment, but prove detrimental to long-term health and happiness. We must satisfy ourselves with an informed outlook that is responsive to health needs rather than temporary indulgences.

and respond when someone says, "Good morning." We may appear apathetic (no interest in development) in a sport when the real problem is some physical condition.[1]

Instructions are very much a part of our motivation, development, and performance, and to ignore them is to introduce needless risks that will likely increase stress, reduce effectiveness, and increase failure. When we most fully appreciate this first Prime Determinant, health and success become a natural part of our lives.

2. The Psychology of Success—Your Natural *Instincts*

D2 - *Instincts* - Natural Tendencies

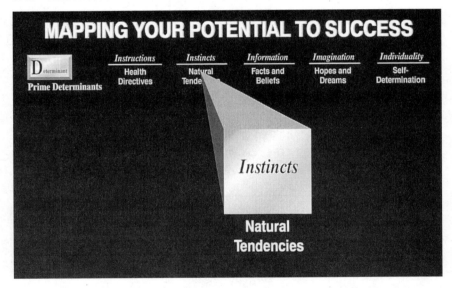

Key element question: "Do people sense the probability of themselves clearly attaining success?"

Instincts are the second Prime Determinant that affect our motivation, development, and performance. *Instincts* are like the basic system software in a computer and contain fixed tendencies for simple operations and survival. How the system responds to outages

---

1. David G. Myers, *Psychology*, 4th ed. (New York: Worth Publishers, 1995), 399.

in electricity or memory protection faults or storage failures is much like how we respond to danger and social difficulties. *Instincts* are an inborn pattern of activity or tendency to action designed to help us react to situations in our lives.[2]

Instincts are innate tendencies for behaving in fixed patterns without the involvement of conscious thought. These *instincts* may include the need to maintain safety (respond appropriately to danger) and security (storing food for the future), as well as to procreate our species through our sexuality.

Without these *instincts* to direct us as social entities, it would take many years to figure out guidelines, rules, and procedures for survival, living together, and raising families. Like *instructions*, *instincts* do not require any conscious thought, even though *instincts* can be influenced by conscious thoughts.

During *instinctual* responses (such as fight or flight, safety, sexuality, inclusion in groups, loving others, and the desire to be loved), our *instructions* are impacted. Heart and breathing rates increase, blood pressure goes up, digestion slows, adrenaline is released, and sensitivities to sight, sound, smell, taste, and touch increase and are ready for immediate response.

The determination to keep trying or the decision to give up may be based upon a psychological response from *instincts* that either help reach the goal or save energy for better opportunities. When a dog is chasing a rabbit and is just a few feet away, it will chase the rabbit until one of them is exhausted. If the rabbit gets far enough away, the dog gives up.[3]

When we view our chances for success to be slim, our *instincts* tell us to give up. We lose our competitive spirit, and we save our energy for a better opportunity, an opportunity that seems to never materialize.

Without *instincts*, we would miss the opportunity for combining the physiological (*instructions*) and psychological (*instincts*) joys in our lives.

---

2. Ibid., 398.
3. Ibid., 271-272.

3. The Principles of Success—Your Acquired *Information*

D3 - *Information* - Facts and Beliefs

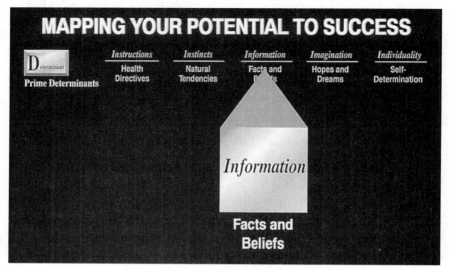

Key element question: "Do people know enough about the expected tasks to ensure success?"

Information is the third Prime Determinant that affects us through our motivation, development, and performance. As an infant, we begin gathering data as a foundation for forming *information*. *Information* is at the center of motivation, development, and performance. What we already know impacts our performance, and what we can learn impacts our development.

Information is the application software part of a computer system which calls up data to produce conclusions that have value and utility. *Information* is made up of **facts and beliefs**. When we lack certain *information*, we form anxiety. Following the death of a loved one, we search our **facts** for answers. When we come up short, we become apprehensive and question the unknowns in our lives, like, "Where is my sister now?" and "Where will I go when I die?" To make up the difference between the amount of **fact** and the amount of *information* we need to avoid anxiety, we form **beliefs** (Figure 26).

Figure 26. **Facts Versus Beliefs**
Increasing our level of **facts** is the surest way to reduce anxiety. We need to test our **beliefs** with structured *information*, so we can answer the questions at the root of our problems.

4. The Possibilities of Success—Your Creative *Imagination*

D4 - *Imagination* - Hopes and Dreams

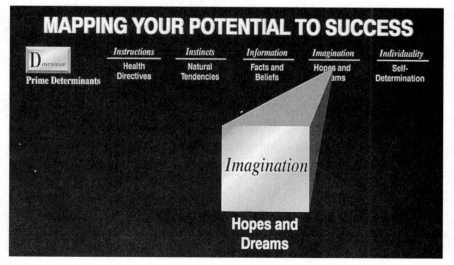

Key element question: "Can people see the possibilities for new results to create more success?"

Imagination is the fourth Prime Determinant that affects our motivation, development, and performance.

Albert Einstein said, *"Imagination is more important than knowledge,"* because *information* is limited by reality, and *imagination* allows for unlimited possibilities, regardless of facts or circumstances.

Imagination is behind the creation of new products, services, and ideas which allow people to refocus their lives to spend more time doing what they want to do. Positive outcomes build on one another and add to our quality of life when we are able to do what we want (as a result of *imagination*).

Our *imagination* can also produce negative outcomes. For example, this can take the form of personal conflicts that are blamed on the "hostility" of others, resulting in paranoia. Negative outcomes build on one another, aggravating our thoughts. At times there may be no balance to check this form of *imagination*; our thinking will degenerate to include less and less reality.

Imagination can be most closely associated with computers which can generate new sentences or images. However, decisions beyond logical, programmed parameters require intuitive judgment which goes beyond dependency upon any reasoning process.

Our *imaginations* can cause or eliminate distress or eustress. We can begin to eliminate distress with a new perspective. How often do people worry about something that is not true or never happens? My audiences estimate that at least 90 percent of the time their fears never materialize. Why should we allow our *imagination* to control us and waste our energies over nothing?

Eustress must be buttressed by reality. A useful exercise is to envision two positive thoughts for every negative thought or consequence you envision. We must put these thoughts into action by calling on the next Prime Determinant.

5. The Personalization of Success—Your Own *Individuality*
D5 - *Individuality* - Self-Determination

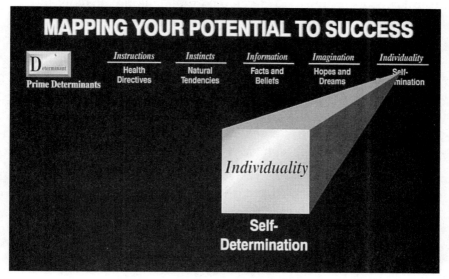

<u>Key element question</u>: "Are people capable of developing their own fulfillment within success?"

Individuality is the fifth Prime Determinant that affects our motivation, development, and performance. This element provides the greatest control over all decisions, beyond any influence from the lower Prime Determinants of human behavior. This Prime Determinant can assist in reducing stress. The degree of control an executive has over his or her organization serves as a buffer against a stress reaction.[4]

If an artist had someone's hand on the back of their hand while painting a picture, how good would that picture be? And how close would the picture come to the artist's original intent? All learning and growth is truly an individual experience of development, even though other people are there to teach and support us. *Individuality* is in charge.

---

4. Richard Restak, M.D., *The Brain* (New York: Bantam Books, 1984), 167-168.

An analogy for how the five Prime Determinants work in our lives can be that of a five-wheeled car. The first four wheels (the first four Prime Determinants) are on the ground taking the daily shocks of potholes and bad weather. These Prime Determinants get out of alignment from time to time. Until we see the real problem of alignment and set the wheels right by making the necessary adjustments, we may spend the rest of our lives straining to pull ourselves back on the road or experiencing mishaps. The fifth wheel is the steering wheel or *individuality*. We are in charge of the vehicle (ourselves). Persons with a low need for *achievement* are content with their present status. Persons with a high need for *achievement* strive to meet a desired level of excellence. This striving is a trait of *individuality*.[5]

The Prime Determinants have given us a perspective on ourselves. This perspective allows us to understand any personal barriers and how to overcome those barriers (Figure 24). This perspective, coupled with the insights we have gained from the Goals, Relationships, and Ideologies classifications, prepares us for taking the Fundamental Steps to Success in chapter 6.

5. Justin Longenecker, Carlos Moore, and J. William Petty, *Small Business Management*, 10th ed. (Cincinnati: South-Western Publishing Company, 1997), 9.

MAPPING YOUR POTENTIAL TO SUCCESS
THE TABLE OF SUCCESS ELEMENTS
WITH KEY ELEMENT QUESTIONS
("No" responses indicate key elements.)

Increasing Participation ← Performance............................Balance............................Development→

	Accomplishment **Maximizing Effectiveness** G1	*Agreement* **Unifying Opinions** G2	*Affiliation* **Forming Bonds** G3	*Affirmation* **Confirming Wholeness** G4	*Achievement* **Ensuring Growth** G5
Goal **Primary Goals** [Equivalent Sets w/R]	Are all routine tasks performed at the expected/ required level of proficiency?	Are people concurring on what and how things need to be done?	Are people working closely together while supporting the overall efforts?	Are people supported in easing burdens and meeting personal needs?	Are people developing new abilities to do what they need to do?
	Management **Synergism** R1	*Marketing* **Selling** R2	*Matching* **Sharing** R3	*Ministry* **Serving** R4	*Mastery* **Skills** R5
Relationship **Basic Relationships** [Equivalent Sets w/G]	Is it impossible for people to enhance their performances by joint efforts?	Are discussions or suggestions satisfying needs and desires of individuals?	Do people's strengths balance and complement each other?	Do people lend support to other people needing self-assurance and direction?	Are people consistently developing their expertise for effectiveness?
	Theory X **Command** I1	Theory Y **Camaraderie** I2	Theory Z **Consensus** I3	Theory M **Confusion** I4	Theory I **Competency** I5
Ideology **Principal Ideologies** [Subsets of Theory I]	Do people know what to do and how to do it without being told to perform?	Do people have the freedom to do what is most meaningful and gratifying?	Do people work cooperatively in support of one another as an effective team?	When people feel job security, do they strive to increase their effectiveness?	Are people fulfilled while developing expertise to be most effective?
	Instructions **Health Directives** D1	*Instincts* **Natural Tendencies** D2	*Information* **Facts and Beliefs** D3	*Imagination* **Hopes and Dreams** D4	*Individuality* **Self-Determination** D5
Determinant **Prime Determinants** [Overlapping Sets]	Are people physically capable and mentally alert for performing?	Do people sense the probability of themselves clearly attaining success?	Do people know enough about the expected tasks to ensure success?	Can people see the possibilities for new results to create more success?	Are people capable of developing their own fulfillment within success?

Chapter 6

THE FUNDAMENTAL STEPS TO SUCCESS

We assimilate Theory *I* knowledge into a plan by addressing: **Introduction to the Fundamental Steps to Success**; **Fundamental Steps, Attributes, and Key Element Questions**; **Implementing the Fundamental Steps to Success**; and **The Table of Success Elements.**

Introduction to the Fundamental Steps to Success

Everything we learn about success is derived from steps (Figure 27). The bottom line of GRIDS comprises the Fundamental Steps to success. How we address the steps is a result of the elements, principles, and strategies of Theory *I*. With GRIDS we can explore our *environment* to the fullest. All *experiences* we have had (or will have) become more meaningful when they aid in producing success. We tie together all of the *elements* (elements here represent all of the elements within Theory *I*) into a complete strategy for success. (The matrix is composed of elements, and it is at this point—the *elements* cell—that all of these elements are injected into the Fundamental Steps.) After constructing this plan for success, we *exercise* ourselves and others involved to the point of ensuring success. Finally, we *experiment* with situations we face to gain the best results through our efforts.

Steps are progressions toward successful completion of a task or job. There are five Fundamental Steps which begin with a clear view of the realm of **opportunities** (what *can* be done) and end with the implementation of strategies to meet those **opportunities**

Figure 27

Our Earliest Choices
Each of us has choices to make
from our very beginnings:
following the footsteps of others,
or taking an uncharted course.
A path of footsteps may appeal to
us early on, but they end at the
water's edge of new
opportunity.

(what *will* be done). Answering the key questions in the Fundamental Step classification will allow you to make informed decisions about **opportunities, challenges, theories, activities,** and **to-do's.**

Before choosing steps in a plan for success, a manager might ask: (1) Do the people involved know how to discover **opportunities** for producing success? (2) Do these people become personally involved in exploring avenues for meeting **challenges**? (3) Do people see both the big and small pictures that make up a blueprint or **theory** for success? (4) Are people practicing **activities** properly to get better at what needs to be done? (5) Do people try **to do** what is most important to produce results? The answers to each of these questions come through taking the Fundamental Steps to success.

In set theory, this class of elements is a *universal set*, which means each element can join with any other appropriate element(s) to form a principle (according to the rules of set theory) and a resulting strategy. If we think of the five levels of the matrix as a hand, with the first four representing fingers, the bottom row is universal and can touch any of the other elements, just as the thumb can touch and interact with each of the fingers. For a diagram of the universal sets in Theory *I*, please see the Fundamental Steps classification in appendix B.

Fundamental Steps, Attributes, and Key Element Questions

S1 - *Environment* - Opportunities—Where Success Is Possible

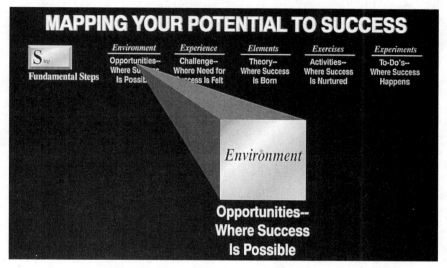

Key element question: "Do people take the simplest route first, to increase their chances for successful performances?"

The first Fundamental Step to success is finding or creating **opportunities**. An **opportunity** is a favorable condition within a situation for attaining a goal. It is the attainment of this goal that leads us to the end result that we seek. Focusing on the attribute for *agreement* (**unifying opinions**) and the attribute for *marketing* (**selling**) creates an **opportunity** which produces an *environment* where the purchase (end result) is possible.

Why do people miss **opportunities**? People are often so busy at work that they have little time to consider **opportunities** outside work. People become driven by electronic or paper in-baskets, phone calls, meetings, and corporate politics. **Opportunities** may be presented to people, conditioning them to weed through stacks of **opportunities** and prioritize them. When people leave their job or retire, the constant flow of **opportunity** stops, and they may not be equipped to face possibilities in their future.

Opportunities in our *environment* become visible through emerging goals, evolving relationships, open communication styles or ideologies, and determinants, such as: increasing alertness (*instructions*), developing a sense of winning (*instincts*), gaining knowledge of available **opportunities** (*information*), creating new ideas (*imagination*), and clarifying decisions to take action (*individuality*). Consider how **opportunities** can arise out of any element such as *agreement* or *disagreement, affiliation* or estrangement, etc. This exploratory exercise will help broaden our perspective on **opportunity**.

Let's suppose you have had a busy week at work. On a Saturday morning your spouse suggests going shopping with the kids, and you agree. As your family is getting into the car, the kids have to run back into the house because they forgot things they wanted to bring, but this does not bother you.

While shopping you see a sign in the window of a store that carries expensive business suits. The sign says, "GOING OUT OF BUSI-NESS," and the mark down is 80 percent. *Information* gets your *instincts* worked up enough to rush in to the store (seize an **opportunity**) to compete with anyone who wants a good bargain in your size. Your *instructions* have your heart pounding as you walk quickly toward the rack of suits for your size. Your *imagination* dreams of how wonderful it will be to buy several suits and how impressed your colleagues and clients will be when you come to work on Monday. You have already decided through your *individuality* that you will definitely buy at least five suits.

When you arrive at your size of suits, all you see is an empty rack; all of the suits in your size are gone. As you are getting ready to leave, empty-handed, you notice a person in line who has a stack of suits. You ask him, "How many suits did you buy?" and he answers, "They were such a bargain, I bought eight." You ask him the size of the suits he bought, and he tells you your size. Then you ask when he got to the store, and it turns out to be about two minutes before you did.

Suddenly you realize that the fact that your children held you up before leaving home has allowed for this **opportunity** to pass you by. Instead of focusing on the real issues of why an **opportunity** was missed, it is common to place blame where it is convenient, regardless of true fault. This scenario demonstrates the need for us to sharpen our skills for discovering or creating **opportunities**. With more **opportunities** to choose from, we will not be devastated when one of them does not pan out, for whatever reason. We will hopefully have many more to choose from.

S2 - *Experiences* - Challenge—Where Need for Success Is Felt

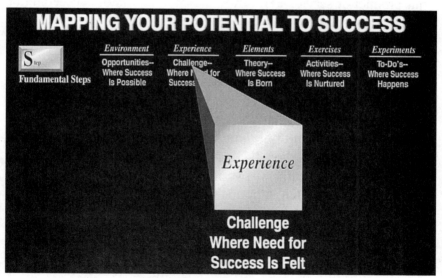

Key element question: "Do people feel they are an important part of what needs to be done to create success?"

Opportunities lie dormant until they become **challenges** to somebody. **Challenges** are personalized slices of **opportunity**. We do not always choose which slice we receive, but we can choose from the different types of goals to produce the end result we seek.

In examining *experience* within the Fundamental Step classification, we look into the dynamics of a **challenge** (the attribute). Suppose you are a sales representative for a company and you have a quota of **selling** 12 units in a year. There are certain tasks you may already know how to perform, such as identifying prospects and explaining the features of your products. To repeat these tasks, you would have a goal of *accomplishment*. Once you make contact with a potential customer, you need to have a goal of *agreement* (assuming that you understand how to market). If you were uncertain about how to meet this end result (the quota), you would need a goal of *achievement*.

At the end of an unproductive day of **selling**, you may sense frustration if your goal had been one of *agreement* (a customer agreeing to buy your product or service). However, the *experiences* of succeeding or failing in producing a sale could be equally rewarding if your goal had been *achievement*. A *mastery* Basic Relationship is formed to develop your abilities (e.g., **selling skills**) to the highest possible level of personal *achievement*. When you fail to meet your goals of *agreement*, the end result is the fulfillment of your goal of *achieving* greater knowledge of how *not* to sell.

Ultimately, if you sold one unit in ten sales calls, you might ask yourself what you said or did in the tenth call that you could have done in the ninth call. Answering this question becomes your **challenge**. The **challenge** is not whether you can *achieve* a goal, but whether can you *achieve* the goal fast enough to meet the expectation of the quota deadline. To continue the example, you become frustrated by a yearly quota you must meet. If someone were to ask you if you could reach this quota in ten years, you would not feel frustration; rather, you would be confident you could *achieve* it. The question is not one of ultimate performance but speed of performance based upon development. Therefore, if you were able to answer the question of what you did on your tenth call to complete the sale, and you used that on your ninth call, you would be able to increase your productivity by ten percent. If you continue to ask this question for the eighth call, seventh call, etc., ultimately you might get your successful call rate down to one call.

S3 - *Elements* - Theory—Where Success Is Born

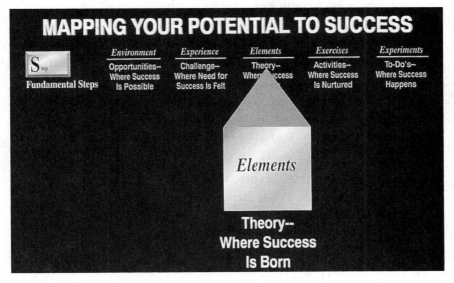

Key element question: "Do people have a perspective for success that is built upon even the smallest key variables?"

A **theory** is what puts all of the smallest pieces (*elements*) together in a meaningful way (based on principles) so that we can see the entire picture before we practice and ultimately *experiment* with alternatives. Practicing a bad golf swing makes no sense; you need someone to show you what you are doing wrong, so you can practice swinging the golf club the right way.

The advantage of a **theory** is that all of the pieces (*elements*) are readily available for consideration in the creation of new strategies. *Elements* have an integral place in shaping our development. An event that happened to me as a child dramatizes what has happened to some degree to all of us regarding our expectations for success, fulfillment, and life in general. This is a story about how curiosity that could have injured me actually provided me with an entirely new perspective on life:

When I was five years old, we lived in a suburb of Cincinnati, Ohio, in a rickety old 19th century house, complete with an old horse barn at the end of the drive. One rainy day, my mother was busy with her sewing machine, my siblings were out for the day, and I was moping through the house, restless and full of energy. I wandered down the upper hall to a door my parents had told me NEVER to open. Gazing at the enormous door, I wondered, "Nobody would know if I opened it just a crack." I reached up and cautiously turned the doorknob. The door sprung open, and I jumped back in fright. But no sound or thing came through the opening.

I peeped around the door. Inside, I saw an amazing room full of old sequined gowns, furs, fancy umbrellas, lots of boxes and walking sticks. What a treasure trove! I pulled down the old clothes and furs, but they did not capture my interest for long, so I started opening the boxes.

Inside one box was a heavy gun and being a naturally curious five-year-old, I pulled the trigger. It clicked—it wasn't loaded. I found the bullets but could not figure out what to do with them, so I went on to explore other things. Inside a leather case was a long, slender object covered by a white cloth with a drawstring. The object was taller than I. When I pulled the string and the cover slid off, I saw a silver eagle, then an ivory handle with the initials "CIS" in fancy lettering— my initials.

I had discovered a highly decorative encasement for a sword. I eagerly pulled out the beautiful, shiny weapon—and in the center of the blade was my name written in fancy bold lettering. I yelled out, "This is MY sword!"

I was so engrossed by this wonderful "gift" that I did not hear my mother approaching, until she screamed at me hysterically, "I told you never to open that door!" With tears streaming down her face, she hugged me and cried, "You could have been killed!"

She marched me down to my room for a serious talk. Mother again explained I was NEVER, NEVER to open that door. When Dad came home she told him about my escapade, and he put a padlock on the door that evening. The incident and the sword became taboo subjects within the family.

While growing up, others heard me describe the sword that was "bigger" than I, much to their amusement as my stature had reached over six feet! At 18, with my mother's permission, I again opened the door to find, to my great disappointment, that the sword had "shrunk." Where was that huge weapon? In my mind, it was still two inches above my head, although in reality it was only 37 inches long. I realized then that my perspective had never changed. Mother told me that my grandfather, whose namesake I was, had carried this ceremonial sword at special Masonic occasions. After a long, painful bout of cancer, he had ended his life with the same gun I had found in the closet. My mother's anger and hysteria so many years ago were now explained.

Exploring why my mother was upset (the *information* she had that I, my grandfather's namesake, had handled his suicide weapon) did not occur to me. My mother's protectiveness of me (her *instinct*) exacerbated her hysterical reaction. My mother became ill with a migraine headache on the evening of the incident, and I did not see her for several days. For many years afterward I envisioned myself as the cause of this pain, and I could not stop *imagining* the suffering she was going through. The chemical reactions (*instructions*) in her body had brought on the headache. Not knowing this, I decided (an act of *individuality*) to do my best to avoid upsetting my mother again.

Beyond the Prime Determinants that were directing my mother's and my actions, there were other *elements* to consider, such as my goal of exploring the closet (*achievement*), my mother's goal of keeping me away from the closet (*accomplishment* of safety), my *mastery* of the situation by fulfilling my goal of opening the closet door, and my mother's *management* to avoid the risk realized through my curiosity. My independent nature made me ignore my mother's wishes and open the door because I wanted to explore. My mother was motivated by the need to take complete control of a dangerous situation (using the ideology of Theory *X*). My **opportunity** was to satisfy my curiosity and meet the **challenge** of exploring the unknown while resisting my mother's authority. I had no methodology to my actions, and because I had not allowed for every possibility, I had in effect exposed myself to danger. My *experiment* was to act and discover what could happen; I had no idea of possible after-effects.

The sword incident became an interesting, broadening perspective for my life, rather than a source of fear as a significant life-shaping event. No longer would unknown elements and principles run my life. No longer would I wait for someone else to lay down the strategy for my life. I remember going back and rereading the Bible inscription my mother had placed on the inside cover of my sixteenth birthday present, my dictionary: "Prove all things. Hold fast to that which is good." That suggestion became a personal **challenge**: to discover what ultimately became the elements, principles, and strategies needed to improve human potential for success.

Damocles was a member of the court of Dionysius II, who ruled Syracuse, Sicily, from 367 to 344 B.C. Damocles talked excessively about the happiness and good fortune of Dionysius. To teach Damocles a lesson, Dionysius invited him to a big feast. Once seated, Damocles looked up and saw a sword, suspended by a single hair, dangling over his head. This precariously hanging sword gave Damocles a new perspective. It reminded him of the constant danger that accompanied the wealth and material happiness of Dionysius. The Damocles' swords from our past can intimidate us, paralyze our thinking, and keep us from pursuing **opportunities**.

"Swords" from the past needlessly hang over us and weaken our belief in ourselves and in our capabilities. The biggest lie we can tell ourselves is, "I am as good as I am ever going to be." Our happiness and wealth are needlessly diminished by these swords. We must use elements of truth to create a theory for achieving our potential.

S4 - *Exercises* - Activities—Where Success Is Nurtured

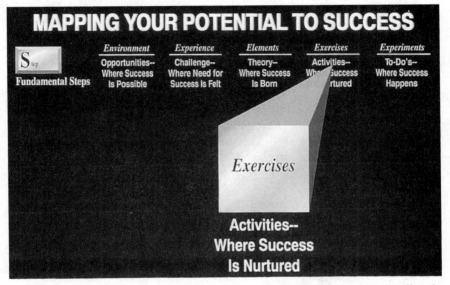

Key element question: "Are people receiving the needed feedback and practice for fine-tuning success?"

Certain *exercises* are not only useless in encouraging growth or development, but some of those *exercises* could cause damage. "Just do it!" may not be wise for some people to follow. Sometimes people get caught up in the aura of false confidence and superficial knowledge, and accept unproven advice that could be harmful. To ensure continuous progress toward success, we need to monitor our *exercises* to ensure that practicing our performance truly makes our performance better.

Sports provide excellent examples for illustrating *exercises* for improvement (Figure 28). To be effective as a diver, the dive must be broken down into phases and examined, just like GRIDS breaks down success into its component parts. What is on a diver's mind is critically important during practice and competition.

Figure 28. **Success Comes One Step at a Time**
U.S. National Champion Diver Doug Shaffer spent years perfecting his
skills. To succeed, we must examine, refine, and practice all of the steps
that lead us to meeting our desired end results.

Success or failure comes moment by moment, often at the blink of
an eye. We may not know what happened; however, the eye of a
trained professional can help. Just as a stop action view of each key
position in a dive reveals success or failure in the making, so it is
with each element and classification of GRIDS. Imagine being
able to perform a stop action clinic in your next encounter with an
employee, a client, a spouse, a friend in need, or yourself developing
your own improvement. A trained eye for success uses each of the
elements within each of the classifications to explain and correct
each of our steps to success.

What determines success? The trained eyes of coaches and judges see "snapshots" of positions as the diver goes through the motions. Using GRIDS we can do the same while practicing for our improvements. Failure at the end of a dive is a symptom of a problem, not the problem. By practicing **activities** using GRIDS we isolate the real problems and develop strategies for real solutions.

S5 - *Experiments* - To-Do's—Where Success Happens

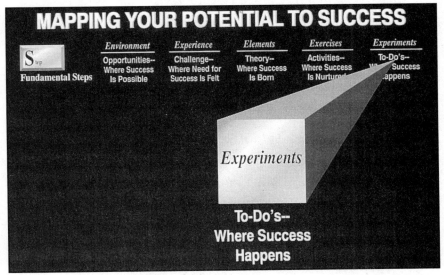

Key element question: "Are people able to develop a strategy for mapping their potential to success?"

Through the Fundamental Steps we can place **opportunity** and **challenge** on our **to-do** list. First, we structure every consideration within a comprehensive, workable **theory**. Next, we practice the necessary **activities**, test the results, and further develop ourselves to do what must be done. The final step is to conduct the **to-do's** that make our success happen.

When people suggest, "Just do it!" they beg the question, "Do what?" It is not unusual for people to wonder about their goals, like Alice wondered where she was headed.

Alice: Would you tell me, please, which way I ought to go from here?

Cheshire Cat: That depends a good deal on where you want to get to.

Alice: I don't much care where—

Cat: Then it doesn't matter which way you go.

Alice: —so long as I get SOMEWHERE.

Cat: Oh, you're sure to do that if you only walk long enough.

Alice: What sort of people live about here?

Cat: In that direction lives a Hatter, and in that direction lives a March Hare. Visit either you like; there're both mad.

Alice: But I don't want to go among mad people.

Cat: Oh, you can't help that, we're all mad here. I'm mad. You're mad.

Alice: How do you know I'm mad?

Cat: You must be or you wouldn't have come here.

— *Alice's Adventures in Wonderland* by Lewis Carroll (Macmillan, London, 1865)

Knowing everything we can possibly know about goals, relationships, ideologies, and determinants is important; however, the final step (*experimenting*) is crucial to making something happen.

Implementing the Fundamental Steps to Success

The attribute of **opportunity** (where success is possible) offers unlimited possibilities. For example, travelers often look for places to dine upon arrival in new locations. Someone needs to answer their questions on how to find a restaurant. This usually falls on registration clerks, who are already quite busy. Oftentimes, neither the clerk nor the traveler is satisfied with the advice. People waiting in line to check in are even less satisfied. Alleviating this problem is the **opportunity**. To accept the **challenge**, we need *experience* (through interviews of patrons of the hotel, registration clerks, and hotel managers) on how to pinpoint and fulfill this need.

Having the **opportunity** and sensing the **challenge**, we are now ready to put all of the pieces together in a **theory** or theoretical model for success that would fulfill each **opportunity** and meet each **challenge**. This may include ideas such as a display rack of wallet-sized menus containing food, prices, hours, and directions to local restaurants. The theoretical model would also detail estimated revenues from participating restaurants and hotels, the costs of creating and distributing the menus, roles of individuals involved, etc.

For an **activity**, we could select different representative situations (for example, three restaurants and three hotels) for testing our model. After this model is *exercised* and proven successful, through feedback and adjustments, we are ready for the final step.

Fully using this working model is the final step. If we are successful, it is time to implement a full-scale operation. Using a **to-do** list, we contact all hotels and restaurants to explain our success in the test models, and invite them to receive similar benefits. We are now ready to satisfy the entire **opportunity** within a given area (city).

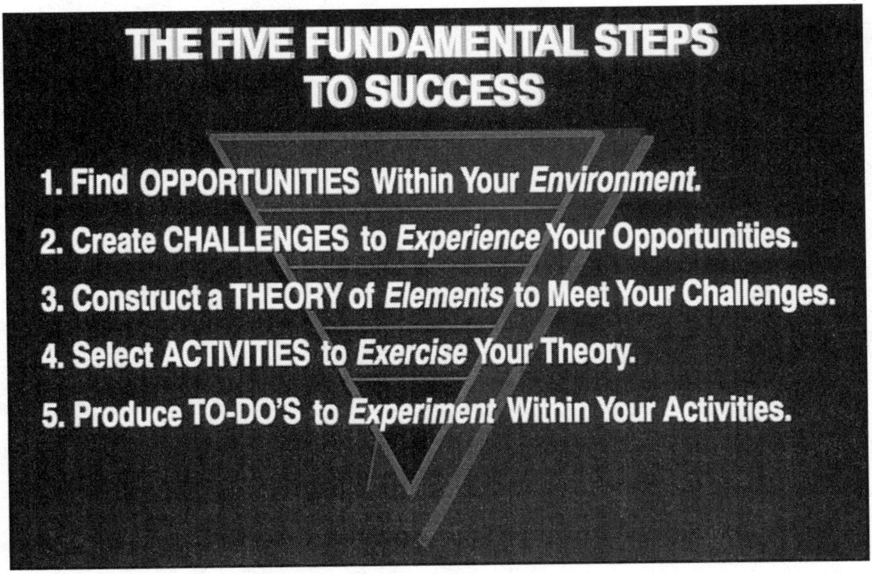

THE FIVE FUNDAMENTAL STEPS TO SUCCESS

1. Find OPPORTUNITIES Within Your *Environment.*

2. Create CHALLENGES to *Experience* Your Opportunities.

3. Construct a THEORY of *Elements* to Meet Your Challenges.

4. Select ACTIVITIES to *Exercise* Your Theory.

5. Produce TO-DO'S to *Experiment* Within Your Activities.

Figure 29

To use the steps (Figure 29) most effectively, we must be prepared to *experiment*. Part of the reward and excitement in any *experiment* is the feedback and the making of needed adjustments along the way.

First, recognize that in conducting an *experiment* mistakes will be made and lessons will be learned. We must also settle in our minds the idea that the greatest value in any single *experiment* may be in learning how something ought not to be done. Thomas Edison reportedly made at least 10,000 attempts to invent the battery. Some sources even claim it was over 40,000 attempts. In either regard, Edison was asked, "Didn't you ever get tired of trying?" He responded, "No, because now I know 10,000 [40,000] ways it will not work."

MAPPING YOUR POTENTIAL TO SUCCESS
THE TABLE OF SUCCESS ELEMENTS
WITH KEY ELEMENT QUESTIONS
("No" responses indicate key elements.)

↓Increasing Participation ←Performance..........................Balance..........................Development→

	Accomplishment **Maximizing Effectiveness** G1	Agreement **Unifying Opinions** G2	Affiliation **Forming Bonds** G3	Affirmation **Confirming Wholeness** G4	Achievement **Ensuring Growth** G5
Goal **Primary Goals** [Equivalent Sets w/R]	Are all routine tasks performed at the expected/required level of proficiency?	Are people concurring on what and how things need to be done?	Are people working closely together while supporting the overall efforts?	Are people supported in easing burdens and meeting personal needs?	Are people developing new abilities to do what they need to do?
	Management **Synergism** R1	Marketing **Selling** R2	Matching **Sharing** R3	Ministry **Serving** R4	Mastery **Skills** R5
Relationship **Basic Relationships** [Equivalent Sets w/G]	Is it impossible for people to enhance their performances by joint efforts?	Are discussions or suggestions satisfying needs and desires of individuals?	Do people's strengths balance and complement each other?	Do people lend support to other people needing self-assurance and direction?	Are people consistently developing their expertise for effectiveness?
	Theory X **Command** I1	Theory Y **Camaraderie** I2	Theory Z **Consensus** I3	Theory M **Confusion** I4	Theory I **Competency** I5
Ideology **Principal Ideologies** [Subsets of Theory I]	Do people know what to do and how to do it without being told to perform?	Do people have the freedom to do what is most meaningful and gratifying?	Do people work cooperatively in support of one another as an effective team?	When people feel job security, do they strive to increase their effectiveness?	Are people fulfilled while developing expertise to be most effective?
	Instructions **Health Directives** D1	Instincts **Natural Tendencies** D2	Information **Facts and Beliefs** D3	Imagination **Hopes and Dreams** D4	Individuality **Self-Determination** D5
Determinant **Prime Determinants** [Overlapping Sets]	Are people physically capable and mentally alert for performing?	Do people sense the probability of themselves clearly attaining success?	Do people know enough about the expected tasks to ensure success?	Can people see the possibilities for new results to create more success?	Are people capable of developing their own fulfillment within success?
	Environment **Opportunities—** Where Success Is Possible S1	Experience **Challenge—** Where Need for Success Is Felt S2	Elements **Theory—** Where Success Is Born S3	Exercises **Activities—** Where Success Is Nurtured S4	Experiments **To-Do's—** Where Success Happens S5
Step **Fundamental Steps** [Universal Sets]	Do people take the simplest route first, to increase their chances for successful performances?	Do people feel they are an important part of what needs to be done to create success?	Do people have a perspective for success that is built upon even the smallest key variables?	Are people receiving the needed feedback and practice for fine-tuning success?	Are people able to develop a strategy for mapping their potential to success?

Chapter 7

APPLYING THE TOOLS AND STRATEGIES OF THEORY *I*

We apply Theory *I* by addressing: **How Theory *I* Strategies Work, How to Use Theory *I*'s Tools and Strategies, The Five Strategies of Theory *I* and OCS Example,** and **Opportunity/Challenge Surveys.**

How Theory *I* Strategies Work

The purpose of a strategy is to satisfy the performer's vision of success by mapping a path from where he or she is now to where he or she needs to go in the future. Strategies are formed by identifying key elements needed to resolve a particular circumstance within a situation. Broader strategies are formed by joining *elements* from different classes within the GRIDS matrix.

For each strategy, only one element may be selected from each of the five classes of *elements*. For example, if more than one goal is needed to produce the desired end result, then another strategy needs to be constructed for each goal. The same applies to relationships, ideologies, determinants, and steps.

How to Use Theory *I*'s Tools and Strategies

There are two tools for using the Theory *I* methodology. Whether we are exploring what we need to learn or applying what we already know, these tools assist in creating different types of strategies which build upon the interaction of *elements*.

1. **Opportunity/Challenge Survey (OCS)** - This exploratory tool uses *elements* to detect and initially guide needed improvements through *single-element strategies*. An example of a completed OCS follows at the end of this chapter and may be helpful in explaining use of this tool and accompanying terminology. To ensure accuracy and thoroughness all OCS statements are based on the key element questions in the GRIDS matrix.

2. **Table of Success Elements (TSE)** - This application tool is the foundation of the OCS. It offers perspective for the creation of comprehensive strategies (*full strategies*). Full strategies address the complete range of element classes defined in GRIDS. TSE is also a guide for *interim strategies* that solve unexpected difficulties discovered in a full strategy. Finally, TSE provides the framework for sequencing all full strategies for greatest benefit through a superstrategy.

Figure 30. **Targeting Success**
Just as the F-22 Advanced Stealth Fighter locks onto a target, we must do the same with **challenges** and **opportunities**. This machine is tuned to achieve its directive, just as a Theory *I* user is prepared for success.

To target your success (Figure 30), you must go through an OCS item by item and rank the statements on a scale from 1-5 (from "disagree" to "agree"). If any item along the way does not apply to your circumstances, mark "5," so it will not later be considered for generating a single-element strategy. Your point of view in responding to each statement is indicated by the personal pronoun used in the statement. [For first person (I or we) statements, consider yourself. For third person (participant or employee) statements, consider the particular people involved.] For any item marked 1-4, highlight the corresponding single-element strategy for later reference. Strategies marked "1" must be addressed first, followed by the "2's" and so forth.

The Five Strategies of Theory *I* and OCS Example

Please refer to the completed OCS example at the end of this chapter (Ex.: SURVEY 1 - pages 132-133). As you can see, there are a number of *elements* that need to be addressed (those with lower than a 5 ranking) to ensure success. To gain the strongest commitments for success from project participants, we need a strategy that satisfies the participants (personal strategy) and the organization (corporate strategy). These two strategies must be combined into one strategy called a *parallel strategy*.

A *parallel strategy* ensures none of the strategies overshadow personal or corporate objectives. Also, all significant barriers are addressed simultaneously (in parallel) for a non-stop resolution within a relatively short period of time.

To be sure we address a problem using all of GRIDS, we need a *full strategy*. A full strategy contains only one element from each GRIDS classification. Each of these *elements* has a corresponding *single-element strategy* on the OCS. If there are two or more key elements within a class, each key element needs its own full strategy. To resolve a problem, there may be a number of *full strategies* necessary. Once all full strategies have been developed, they are sequenced into a *superstrategy*.

Referring to Ex.: SURVEY 1, we rank R1 at "1." This tells us the "Project leader is NOT enhancing performances of participants by coordinating their joint efforts." There may be a number of reasons why a project leader ranked R1 as a "1." Perhaps the project leader did not coordinate due to an oversight; or the project leader has not had enough experience in coordinating.

An oversight would be most easily addressed with the R1 single-element strategy that reminds the project leader to "Have everyone perform what they do best to promote increased **synergism**." This single-element strategy would be built into a full strategy, incorporating one element from each class.

Lack of experience would warrant an *interim strategy* beginning with a G5 goal of *achievement* for the project leader to "Develop a new level of results by **ensuring growth**," and an R5 relationship of *mastery* to "Develop critical **skills** to assure effectiveness for increasing individual qualifications." This interim strategy would continue by addressing the appropriate ideology, determinant, and step. Elaborating upon the final GRIDS classification, the step may be S2 for gaining *experience* in other smaller **challenges**, or S4 for using *exercises* to simulate experience through **activities**. Once this interim strategy is completed, the project leader will be able to resume the full strategy beginning with the R1 single-element strategy to "Have everyone perform what they do best to promote increased **synergism**."

Let's examine the first scenario, where the lack of coordination represents an oversight on the part of the project leader. Since we begin with the lowest ranked OCS responses first, we would start with the "1" in G1. G1 requires an R1 because they are an equivalent set. With this set theory rule, the first statement [G1] says, "Project participants perform all routine tasks at the expected/required level of proficiency." The single-level strategy would be: "Refine and perfect routine tasks...[so that project participants can] perform with **maximum effectiveness**."

OPPORTUNITY/CHALLENGE SURVEY

Ex.: SURVEY 1 - Project Leader: *Exploratory Tool for Producing Single-Element Strategies*

Keep a particular symptom of a problem in mind while considering statements and perspectives. Rank statements and perspectives by filling in solid circles covering "1" (disagree) through "5" (agree). Apply needed single-element strategies.

| 1 = totally disagree | 2 = mostly disagree | 3 = inconclusive | 4 = mostly agree | 5 = totally agree |

C #	Successful Project Leader's Statements & Perspectives	Personal Ranking	Successful Project Leader's Single-Element Strategies
G1	Project participants perform all routine tasks at the expected/required level of proficiency.	●-2-3-4-5	Refine and perfect routine tasks to perform with **maximum effectiveness**.

We must go further down the GRIDS matrix to increase our participation in resolving this matter. In our example, the second OCS statement [R1] reads "Project leader enhances performances of participants by coordinating their joint efforts." The single-element strategy would then be to "Have everyone perform what they do best to promote increased **synergism**."

OPPORTUNITY/CHALLENGE SURVEY

Ex.: SURVEY 1 - Project Leader: *Exploratory Tool for Producing Single-Element Strategies*

Keep a particular symptom of a problem in mind while considering statements and perspectives. Rank statements and perspectives by filling in solid circles covering "1" (disagree) through "5" (agree). Apply needed single-element strategies.

| 1 = totally disagree | 2 = mostly disagree | 3 = inconclusive | 4 = mostly agree | 5 = totally agree |

C #	Successful Project Leader's Statements & Perspectives	Personal Ranking	Successful Project Leader's Single-Element Strategies
G1	Project participants perform all routine tasks at the expected/required level of proficiency.	●-2-3-4-5	Refine and perfect routine tasks to perform with **maximum effectiveness**.
R1	Project leader enhances performances of participants by coordinating their joint efforts.	●-2-3-4-5	Have everyone perform what they do best to promote increased **synergism**.

To gain the cooperation of project participants to carry out the above described single-element strategies, the project leader needs to decide upon the most appropriate ideology or communication style.

In our scenario we will assume that we know the **competency** of the participants for performing routine tasks is strong. We also know that they need strong leadership to make a decision on what must be *accomplished* and when it must be completed. Therefore, the ideology of I5 with a subset of I1 (Theory I_x) would be appropriate because we believe the employees not to be self-starters. This ideology combines known **competency** with a **commanding** insistence for specific action.

When I5 is designated as the Principal Ideology, any subset can be considered appropriate. An example documenting the particulars for combining single-element strategies is provided on page 146.

Please note that in our example OCS, I5 has a ranking of "1." Our decision to include I5 in our scenario's full strategy is based upon solving the G1 problem; we are not attempting to address the low ranking of I5. A separate full strategy is needed to address the low opinion that "Project participants are NOT being fulfilled while developing expertise to be most effective."

OPPORTUNITY/CHALLENGE SURVEY
Ex.: SURVEY 1 - Project Leader: *Exploratory Tool for Producing Single-Element Strategies*

Keep a particular symptom of a problem in mind while considering statements and perspectives. Rank statements and perspectives by filling in solid circles covering "1" (disagree) through "5" (agree). Apply needed single-element strategies.

1 = totally disagree	2 = mostly disagree	3 = inconclusive	4 = mostly agree	5 = totally agree

C #	Successful Project Leader's Statements & Perspectives	Personal Ranking	Successful Project Leader's Single-Element Strategies
G1	Project participants perform all routine tasks at the expected/required level of proficiency.	●-2-3-4-5	Refine and perfect routine tasks to perform with **maximum effectiveness**.
R1	Project leader enhances performances of participants by coordinating their joint efforts.	●-2-3-4-5	Have everyone perform what they do best to promote increased **synergism**.
I5	Project participants are being fulfilled while developing expertise to be most effective.	●-2-3-4-5	Develop self through new **competencies** in attaining personal and corporate results.

In our scenario, the reason employees are not performing, and the project leader is not coordinating their actions properly, may be that the employees feel the probability of success in their endeavor is slim as indicated in D2.

OPPORTUNITY/CHALLENGE SURVEY
Ex.: SURVEY 1 - Project Leader: *Exploratory Tool for Producing Single-Element Strategies*

Keep a particular symptom of a problem in mind while considering statements and perspectives. Rank statements and perspectives by filling in solid circles covering "1" (disagree) through "5" (agree). Apply needed single-element strategies.

1 = totally disagree	2 = mostly disagree	3 = inconclusive	4 = mostly agree	5 = totally agree

C #	Successful Project Leader's Statements & Perspectives	Personal Ranking	Successful Project Leader's Single-Element Strategies
G1	Project participants perform all routine tasks at the expected/required level of proficiency.	●-2-3-4-5	Refine and perfect routine tasks to perform with **maximum effectiveness**.
R1	Project leader enhances performances of participants by coordinating their joint efforts.	●-2-3-4-5	Have everyone perform what they do best to promote increased **synergism**.
I5	Project participants are being fulfilled while developing expertise to be most effective.	●-2-3-4-5	Develop self through new **competencies** in attaining personal and corporate results.
D2	Project participants sense a good probability that their efforts will produce success.	●-2-3-4-5	Encourage **natural tendencies** for seeking success by displaying favorable options.

The project leader needs a comprehensive **theory** in his full strategy. It so happens that [S3] was ranked "1," indicating that, "Project participants DO NOT have a complete perspective on variables for overall corporate/personal success." Thus, we implement its corresponding single-element strategy, "Produce a complete picture of the road to success through a comprehensive **theory**." In this case, now that we are at the bottom line of GRIDS, we satisfy both the low-ranking OCS response to S3 and the full strategy simultaneously.

OPPORTUNITY/CHALLENGE SURVEY
Ex.: SURVEY 1 - Project Leader: *Exploratory Tool for Producing Single-Element Strategies*

Keep a particular symptom of a problem in mind while considering statements and perspectives. Rank statements and perspectives by filling in solid circles covering "1" (disagree) through "5" (agree). Apply needed single-element strategies.

1 = totally disagree	2 = mostly disagree	3 = inconclusive	4 = mostly agree	5 = totally agree

C #	Successful Project Leader's Statements & Perspectives	Personal Ranking	Successful Project Leader's Single-Element Strategies
G1	Project participants perform all routine tasks at the expected/required level of proficiency.	●-2-3-4-5	Refine and perfect routine tasks to perform with **maximum effectiveness**.
R1	Project leader enhances performances of participants by coordinating their joint efforts.	●-2-3-4-5	Have everyone perform what they do best to promote increased **synergism**.
I5	Project participants are being fulfilled while developing expertise to be most effective.	●-2-3-4-5	Develop self through new **competencies** in attaining personal and corporate results.
D2	Project participants sense a good probability that their efforts will produce success.	●-2-3-4-5	Encourage **natural tendencies** for seeking success by displaying favorable options.
S3	Project participants have a complete perspective on variables for overall corporate/personal success.	●-2-3-4-5	Produce a complete picture of the road to success through a comprehensive **theory**.

[G1→R1→I5→D2→S3]

To be certain each full strategy is executed as we intended, we sequence each full strategy into a superstrategy.

When unexpected difficulties occur on the way to completing a successful strategy, an interim strategy to solve those difficulties may be necessary. Solution of the interim strategy will keep progress of the overall solution on track. Suppose the project leader did not have the necessary experience for executing the G1 and R1 single-element strategies. Depending upon the circumstances, the interim strategy could include G5 and R5 to focus the project leader on **"ensuring growth"** and "developing critical **skills**," respectively.

The ideology would be selected based upon current **competency** [I5] and the particular needs of the project leader. The project leader's manager needs to consider the style of communication that would work best with this project leader. Such decisions are based on assumptions and judgment. We must consider which of the following examples would obtain the most favorable response:

---

1. **command** $[I_X]$ — "Based upon your current understanding, here is your assignment for learning and when it is expected to be completed," or

2. **camaraderie** $[I_Y]$ — "We have a number of options for you to consider for learning important information, so please tell me which option interests you the most and when you expect to complete it," or

3. **consensus** $[I_Z]$ — "Please work with these other project leaders and discover what makes them successful through observation, discussions, and joint efforts with them," or

4. **confusion** $[I_M]$ — "I prefer for you to perform your duties as I have described; although, I am open to your ideas, and I suggest you work with other project leaders to pick up some of their ideas as well," or

5. **competency** $[I]$ — "Based upon your demonstrated **skills** and knowledge on this particular project, what further developmental support do you need through education, on-the-job training, assistance, or periodic consultation?"

Next, we need to consider which of the following Prime Determinants explain why this project leader is not effective in having participants "perform all routine tasks at the expected/required level of proficiency."

---

1. **health directives** - [D1] Project participant(s) may be ill, or

2. **natural tendencies** - [D2] Participant(s) may have low confidence in producing success based upon past failures, or

---

3. **facts and beliefs** - [D3] The project leader or participants may not be interpreting the facts the same way, making for divergent beliefs and approaches, or

4. **hopes and dreams** - [D4] With recent major changes within the organization, project participant(s) may be discouraged and sense the future appears dim for them, or

5. **self-determination** - [D5] Work may appear to benefit only the organization and work against the career development of the project participant(s).

Finally, we need to examine the steps. Participant(s) or a significant pace setter could be having difficulty regarding:

1. **opportunities** - [S1] There are tasks being ignored that could increase the chances of success (e.g., final checks for errors), or

2. **challenge** - [S2] The involvement of participant(s) is limited because no one has genuinely solicited their help in such a way that makes them feel accountable, or

3. **theory** - [S3] The big picture of how the project comes together and the significance of each part has never been explained or appreciated; therefore, no urgency is sensed by the participant(s), or

4. **activities** - [S4] Without meaningful feedback, participant(s) cannot make appropriate adjustments for improving practice, or

5. **to-do's** - [S5] When change occurs without a strategy, it is common practice for participant(s) to wait to be told to do routine tasks.

In response to all of the above considerations, an interim strategy could be comprised of a development goal of *achievement* [G5], a development relationship of *mastery* [R5], a development ideology of Theory *I* [I5], a performance and development determinant of *information* [D3], and a performance and development step of *elements* [S3], explaining how success can occur, given everything that is needed.

This interim strategy would appear as:

$$G5 \rightarrow R5 \rightarrow I5 \rightarrow D3 \rightarrow S3$$

or as the following chart:

OPPORTUNITY/CHALLENGE SURVEY

Ex.: SURVEY 1 - Project Leader: *Exploratory Tool for Producing Single-Element Strategies*

Keep a particular symptom of a problem in mind while considering statements and perspectives. Rank statements and perspectives by filling in solid circles covering "1" (disagree) through "5" (agree). Apply needed single-element strategies.

1 = totally disagree   2 = mostly disagree   3 = inconclusive   4 = mostly agree   5 = totally agree

C #	Successful Project Leader's Statements & Perspectives	Personal Ranking	Successful Project Leader's Single-Element Strategies
G5	Project participants are developing new abilities to do what they need to do to ensure success.	●-2-3-4-5	Develop a new level of results by **ensuring growth**.
R5	Project participants are consistently developing their expertise for effectiveness in the project.	●-2-3-4-5	Develop critical **skills** to assure effectiveness for increasing individual qualifications.
I5	Project participants are being fulfilled while developing expertise to be most effective.	●-2-3-4-5	Develop self through new **competencies** in attaining personal and corporate results.
D3	Project participants know about the expected tasks and abilities to ensure project success.	1-●-3-4-5	Encourage learning of certain **facts/beliefs** to understand the requirements for success.
S3	Project participants have a complete perspective on variables for overall corporate/personal success.	●-2-3-4-5	Produce a complete picture of the road to success through a comprehensive **theory**.

When the interim strategy is completed, the project leader can go back to the full strategy and remain on track. Another option for an interim strategy may be to hire an assistant or a temporary replacement for the project leader until the interim strategy is completed.

Summary: The following depiction of a strategy shows how this interim strategy becomes embedded within a full strategy. For any statement rated 1-4 in the OCS, users need to select *single-element strategies* (strategies which produce individual results without the support of any other element). Increasing the power of any single-element strategy requires a *full strategy* (participation of all levels of GRIDS). Along the way to creating a full strategy, there are occasions where an *interim strategy* (bracketed below) may be necessary. Why? As we saw, for example, a project leader had a need for certain **skills** in order to *manage,* "...enhance performances of people by coordinating their joint efforts." (See R1 in Ex.: SURVEY 1.)

$$G1 \rightarrow R1 \rightarrow [G5 \rightarrow R5 \rightarrow I5 \rightarrow D3 \rightarrow S3] \rightarrow I5 \rightarrow D2 \rightarrow S3$$

Opportunity/Challenge Surveys

There are eight models of OCS in this text. You may select an OCS based on your status as a project leader, manager, employee, student, etc. Or, you can create your own OCS (a blank OCS is included for this purpose) from these models. Statements for individually tailored OCS's should be derived from the subject matter of the key element questions listed in the Table of Success Elements. Please see appendix C for all models of OCS.

OPPORTUNITY/CHALLENGE SURVEY
Ex.: SURVEY 1 - Project Leader: *Exploratory Tool for Producing Single-Element Strategies*

Keep a particular symptom of a problem in mind while considering statements and perspectives. Rank statements and perspectives by filling in solid circles covering "1" (disagree) through "5" (agree). Apply needed single-element strategies.

1 = totally disagree   2 = mostly disagree   3 = inconclusive   4 = mostly agree   5 = totally agree

C #	Successful Project Leader's Statements & Perspectives	Personal Ranking	Successful Project Leader's Single-Element Strategies
G1	Project participants perform all routine tasks at the expected/required level of proficiency.	●-2-3-4-5	Refine and perfect routine tasks to perform with **maximum effectiveness**.
G2	Project participants concur with project leader/client on what and how things need to be done.	1-2-●-4-5	Discover rationale for differences, and work to **unify opinions** for mutual benefit.
G3	Project participants/clients/management work closely together in support of the overall efforts.	1-●-3-4-5	Create a sincere partnership that results in **forming bonds** with the people involved.
G4	If work becomes overwhelming, project participants can get themselves back on track.	1-2-3-4-●	Assign appropriately sized tasks/responsibilities to encourage confidence and **confirm wholeness**.
G5	Project participants are developing new abilities to do what they need to do to ensure success.	●-2-3-4-5	Develop a new level of results by **ensuring growth**.
R1	Project leader enhances performances of participants by coordinating their joint efforts.	●-2-3-4-5	Have everyone perform what they do best to promote increased **synergism**.
R2	Discussions/suggestions provide valuable ideas supporting needs/desires of project participants.	1-●-3-4-5	Build acceptance of new ideas or concepts through thoroughness in personal **selling**.
R3	The strengths and weaknesses of project participants balance and complement each other.	1-2-●-4-5	Accommodate weaknesses with strengths through **sharing** of self.
R4	Project participants are not in need of support for self-assurance or personal direction.	1-2-3-4-●	Create confidence and self assurance while **serving** other people's needs.
R5	Project participants are consistently developing their expertise for effectiveness in the project.	●-2-3-4-5	Develop critical **skills** to assure effectiveness for increasing individual qualifications.

I1	Project participants know what to do and how to do it without being told to perform.	●-2-3-4-5	Use clear **commands** to require all tasks to be performed properly.
I2	Project participants have the freedom to work at what is most meaningful and gratifying to them.	1-2-3-●-5	Encourage freedoms and satisfaction while working in an atmosphere of **camaraderie**.
I3	Project participants work cooperatively in support of one another as an effective team.	1-2-3-●-5	Bring working people together through overall **consensus**.
I4	When project participants feel job security, they still strive to improve their abilities/effectiveness.	1-●-3-4-5	Replace complacency with **confusion** requiring accountability and self-reliance for self-assurance.
I5	Project participants are being fulfilled while developing expertise to be most effective.	●-2-3-4-5	Develop self through new **competencies** in attaining personal and corporate results.
D1	Project participants are physically capable and mentally alert for performing work every day.	1-●-3-4-5	Ensure a strong performance by building upon **health directives**.
D2	Project participants sense a good probability that their efforts will produce success.	●-2-3-4-5	Encourage **natural tendencies** for seeking success by considering favorable options.
D3	Project participants know about the expected tasks/abilities needed to ensure project success.	1-●-3-4-5	Encourage learning of certain **facts/beliefs** to understand the requirements for success.
D4	Project participants see possibilities for quality/productivity through increasing effectiveness.	1-●-3-4-5	Turn negative thinking and feelings into positive **hopes and dreams**.
D5	Project participants are developing their own sense of responsibility/control over success.	1-●-3-4-5	Encourage **self-determination** to develop personal fulfillment within corporate success.
S1	Project participants take the simplest route to increase chances for performance success.	1-2-●-4-5	Identify and evaluate **opportunities** for potential performance.
S2	Project participants feel a part of what needs to be done to create personal/corporate success.	1-2-3-●-5	Use **challenges** to create involvement and appreciation for what needs to be done.
S3	Project participants have a complete perspective on variables for overall corporate/personal success.	●-2-3-4-5	Produce a complete picture of the road to success through a comprehensive **theory**.
S4	Project participants are receiving the needed feedback/practice for fine-tuning their efforts.	1-●-3-4-5	To create critical proficiencies, incorporate new, meaningful ideas when practicing **activities**.
S5	Project participants are able to develop a total strategy for mapping their potential to success.	1-●-3-4-5	Develop orchestrated **to-do** lists for mapping each venture for success.

MAPPING YOUR POTENTIAL TO SUCCESS
THE TABLE OF SUCCESS ELEMENTS
WITH KEY ELEMENT QUESTIONS
("No" responses indicate key elements.)

↓Increasing Participation ←Performance...................................Balance...........................Development→

	Accomplishment **Maximizing Effectiveness** G1	*Agreement* **Unifying Opinions** G2	*Affiliation* **Forming Bonds** G3	*Affirmation* **Confirming Wholeness** G4	*Achievement* **Ensuring Growth** G5
Goal **Primary Goals** [Equivalent Sets w/R]	Are all routine tasks performed at the expected/ required level of proficiency?	Are people concurring on what and how things need to be done?	Are people working closely together while supporting the overall efforts?	Are people supported in easing burdens and meeting personal needs?	Are people developing new abilities to do what they need to do?
	Management **Synergism** R1	*Marketing* **Selling** R2	*Matching* **Sharing** R3	*Ministry* **Serving** R4	*Mastery* **Skills** R5
Relationship **Basic Relationships** [Equivalent Sets w/G]	Is it impossible for people to enhance their performances by joint efforts?	Are discussions or suggestions satisfying needs and desires of individuals?	Do people's strengths balance and complement each other?	Do people lend support to other people needing self-assurance and direction?	Are people consistently developing their expertise for effectiveness?
	Theory X **Command** I1	*Theory Y* **Camaraderie** I2	*Theory Z* **Consensus** I3	*Theory M* **Confusion** I4	*Theory I* **Competency** I5
Ideology **Principal Ideologies** [Subsets of Theory *I*]	Do people know what to do and how to do it without being told to perform?	Do people have the freedom to do what is most meaningful and gratifying?	Do people work cooperatively in support of one another as an effective team?	When people feel job security, do they strive to increase their effectiveness?	Are people fulfilled while developing expertise to be most effective?
	Instructions **Health Directives** D1	*Instincts* **Natural Tendencies** D2	*Information* **Facts and Beliefs** D3	*Imagination* **Hopes and Dreams** D4	*Individuality* **Self-Determination** D5
Determinant **Prime Determinants** [Overlapping Sets]	Are people physically capable and mentally alert for performing?	Do people sense the probability of themselves clearly attaining success?	Do people know enough about the expected tasks to ensure success?	Can people see the possibilities for new results to create more success?	Are people capable of developing their own fulfillment within success?
	Environment Opportunities— Where Success Is Possible S1	*Experience* Challenge— Where Need for Success Is Felt S2	*Elements* Theory— Where Success Is Born S3	*Exercises* Activities— Where Success Is Nurtured S4	*Experiments* To-Do's— Where Success Happens S5
Step **Fundamental Steps** [Universal Sets]	Do people take the simplest route first, to increase their chances for successful performances?	Do people feel they are an important part of what needs to be done to create success?	Do people have a perspective for success that is built upon even the smallest key variables?	Are people receiving the needed feedback and practice for fine-tuning success?	Are people able to develop a strategy for mapping their potential to success?

Chapter 8

SUMMARY OF THEORY *I*

We expand our application capabilities by addressing: **Bridging Activities that Impact Our Futures, The Five Principles of Theory *I*,** and **Formulation of the Theory *I* Methodology.**

Bridging Activities that Impact Our Futures

There are times when even the simplest path to change and success is ignored because of impassable roadblocks. There are times when we stubbornly refuse to follow the simple path, because we do not want to change for whatever reason.

Whatever we *accomplish* for an organization, the organization owns. We were paid a salary or commission for the results we produced. However, we own the **skills** we developed (through *achievement*) to produce those results. Which has greater value: what we have already done, or what we can do? Since what we can do offers the greatest value, we must learn to expand the value of our **skills**. Our motivation, development, and performance improves because we have adapted the lessons of the past for use in our future. The intent of structured processes is to take everyone to a new level of personal understanding and professional attainment.

When needs remain the same and are routinely satisfied, growth and development stop. Since routine efforts rarely are capable of satisfying new **challenges**, we are in a quandary when those new **challenges** arise. When people demand more from us, we must develop ourselves to new levels of performance that exceed their expectations. Over time, each of us becomes "comfortable" with this new level of performance. We satisfy our needs and other peoples' needs that we consider to be reasonable.

Without **challenge**, most **opportunities** would likely never have been realized. When we contemplate how to meet **challenges**, we rely on Theory *I* for the examination (elements), analysis (principles), and action (strategy) to produce the results we seek. There are many examples of people who have re-dedicated themselves with a new sense of purpose when they were faced with illness, the threat of death, and the hopelessness of poverty. Everyone can be inspired by the triumphs of **challenged** persons; however, we need Theory *I* to attain something meaningful with that inspiration.

"What have you done for me lately?" is a common refrain of people around us who have needs (business and personal). Theory *I* addresses evolving needs by first establishing the right goal. Business competition grows yearly, so the capabilities of people in competing companies must grow too. Customers' needs grow continuously, so new features and services must grow simultaneously. Spousal relationships go through stages: beginning with newlyweds and advancing to parents, empty-nesters, and retirees. Growth is necessary at each stage.

Suppose we were managers, employees, salespeople, customers, or spouses who felt we were making little or no progress, and we were at our wit's end. What are our options? We could nudge the person we are dealing with in new directions, hoping for gradual change. We could also demand change, hoping that the other person will back down and yield to our wishes. When all else fails, we may take a new route that bridges us to **activities** that build strength of character and new **skills**—we can change ourselves. Once we conquer our problems, we can encourage others to take a similar course of action.

Selling another person on the needs, advantages, and benefits of change is dependent upon their confidence, strengths, priorities, and fundamental interests. We can either be patient with what we feel are others' shortcomings, or we can develop our personal strengths to better deal with the disagreeing party. When someone else lets us down, we must build ourselves up to where their weakness interferes less with our success. The stronger and more self-sufficient we become, the less bothersome they can potentially be to us. A much happier and healthier relationship is built by realizing strengths rather than catering to weaknesses or building dependencies.

The Five Principles of Theory *I*

To absorb all of the concepts within the Theory *I* methodology, we have five principles that relate directly to the five classifications of elements. After we decide on a desirable end result, we begin with goals to take us to our destination. Knowing all of the Primary Goals provides a sense of total awareness and confidence that is at the foundation of any professional endeavor.

By bringing people into the right Basic Relationship with each carefully selected goal, we increase our participation in reaching the end result. Within each relationship we must use Principal Ideologies to make the most appropriate assumptions for gaining people's commitments. Personal involvement becomes more thoroughly defined as we examine the Prime Determinants of each person involved in our success. Finally, through precise selection of the Fundamental Steps we complete our journey to success.

The Five Principles of Theory *I*

1. We plan to do our best when we choose from the five Primary Goals that assure success.

2. We jointly do our best when we understand the five Basic Relationships that influence people.

3. We encourage others to do their best when we practice one of the five Principal Ideologies for inspiring people.

4. We personally do our best when we call upon the five Prime Determinants of human behavior.

5. We embark on a journey to do our best when we begin taking the five Fundamental Steps to success.

Formulation of the Theory *I* Methodology

Theory *I* concepts are based on the Theory *I* Table of Success Elements. This comprehensive system of elements, principles, and strategies maintains integrity and merit at all levels of understanding for the requirements of success. Theory *I* identifies the smallest pieces of significant data and gradually builds meaning until they become part of an overall strategy for success.

Data becomes more valuable when properly placed in formation with other data to form *information*: a combination that is far greater in value than the sum of its individual parts. Theory *I* methodology allows for similar exponential growth; it enables us to atomize, reconfigure, and make fruitful any ideas on the subject of success.

Theory *I* turns awareness of what we know and need to know into what we can do and will be able to do in the future. When we can define more precisely what something is and what it is not, we have the rudiments for making more intelligent decisions. In Theory *I*, these rudiments are described as elements. These elements are combined into principles using the rules of set theory within the Theory *I* Table of Success Elements. The rules applied in conjunction with these elements form the principles of Theory *I*.

To examine what we can do, we formulate strategies through the use of elements and principles to address meaningful **challenges** and **opportunities**. To stretch ourselves beyond our past performances, we need tools that allow us to carefully consider every variable (element), every meaningful composition of those variables (principles), and all sensible plans (strategies) to use those variables and compositions to create success. That is why Theory *I*'s comprehensive methodology ultimately creates success in each given situation.

When employing Theory *I*, the only reason we consistently fail is when we inadvertently ignore the elements that guide us to success. Theory *I* provides specific feedback (elements), detailed suggestions for favorable new directions (principles), and tailored alternative plans (strategies) for creating success.

By understanding the formula at the nucleus of Theory *I*, we can far better embrace, apply, and add the value of any truth to our lives. Through Theory *I* we learned to focus our attention on all of the supporting attributes that produce *accomplishment, agreement, affiliation, affirmation,* and *achievement*.

$$\text{ACTIVITY} = \frac{\text{MIND}}{\text{MATTER}}$$

Activity = Mind/Matter is the success equation at the center of Theory *I*. What is on our mind will matter to us in both the immediate and long-range future, because it directly impacts everything we do (**activities**), whether it is a failure or a success. The greater the difference between what we have on our MIND and what already MATTERS, the greater effort (ACTIVITY) we will need to make to balance the equation.

As a practical understanding and application of the Mind over Matter formula, we need to go to the GRIDS chart and ask ourselves questions about what really MATTERS (Primary Goals) and our ACTIVITIES (Basic Relationships). What MATTERS governs what should be on our MINDS (attributes).

To ensure we develop ourselves to produce success, we must employ all three Theory *I* components that were present when this methodology was created. The three components are:

1. MIND - What is on our mind leads us to success or failure. In Theory *I* we focus on the attributes that lead us to efforts that produce the results we seek. When we are confused or ambivalent, people often tell us, "Make up your mind." There are a wide variety of mind-sets for success. Through set theory and the Table of

Success Elements, the Theory *I* methodology allows us to consistently create a mind-set of relevant attributes for any situation.

2. MATTER - What matters to us are the elements that make up the class of Primary Goals. With respect to success, reaching goals matters very much. In fact, people often inadvertently focus on what matters to them—the reward for their efforts. This focus most often generates failure. Through Theory *I* we can change our focus to the attributes that create success.

We have our strongest feelings over the things that matter most. The facts we need to discuss are best defined through the Theory *I* elements for goals. Whether or not we reach our goals truly matters. If we are to produce an *accomplishment*, or an *agreement*, or *affiliation*, or *affirmation*, or an *achievement*, we must be able to form the corresponding relationship between the elements that lead us to resolving critical issues. When we identify what really matters and what affects what matters, we can better address the **challenges** and **opportunities** we face.

3. ACTIVITY - Our MIND and MATTER are impacted by our ACTIVITIES. **Activities** are reflective of the roles we play in our Basic Relationships.

We have *management*, *marketing*, *matching*, *ministry*, and *mastery* **activities** (see Figure 31). The larger the disparity between what is on our minds (the attributes required for producing success) and what matters (the goal), the greater the effort required within our respective **activities**.

When we enter into an ACTIVITY (Basic Relationship), we interact with others. To communicate with and gain the cooperation of others, we make assumptions about how they will respond. The five choices of assumptions are defined within the Principal Ideologies. The Prime Determinants go further into understanding each person as an individual, so we can draw from their unique capabilities to support our chosen **activities**. The Fundamental Steps outline the path for fulfilling our **opportunities** and **challenges**. Structuring key elements and practicing appropriate **activities** are vital to this

Figure 31. **Using the Theory *I* Success Equation**
Focusing on what should be on our minds (attributes) will help us attain what really matters to us (our goals).

process. Eventually, we have practiced our **activities** enough and are ready to *experiment*, guided by a **to-do** list.

Mind over matter is an essential concept for keeping us in touch with who we are (the events and resulting matters that have shaped our identities) and who we can become (our visions of our potentials). Aligning this potential with our performance requires the Theory *I* methodology to guide us from our goals down through our **to-do's** to make success happen. Success is ensured as a result of the following questions and answers:

Which results assure success?......................The Five Primary Goals
How do people influence each other?..The Five Basic Relationships
When are people most effective?.........The Five Principal Ideologies
What affects human behavior?.............The Five Prime Determinants
Where does success begin?...................The Five Fundamental Steps

To increase your familiarity with Theory *I* you may wish to separately or jointly participate in the Theory *I* Exercise in appendix A.

With Theory *I*, we never need to worry about what lies in the future. After completing these eight chapters, your potential for success is infinite. Your mind now focuses on the methodology that makes success a certainty. The italicized elements remind you about what to examine and consider when seeking success. The bolded attributes provide a focus for what leads you to creating success. Now when you contemplate accomplishment, agreement, affiliation, affirmation, or achievemnent, these words and their attributes, even without special treatment of italicization or bolding, will jump out in forming principles to guide you in formulating strategies for whatever you decide to do. Theory *I* is your theory. There is no limit to your success.

☐☐☐☐☐ THE THEORY *I* EXERCISE ☐☐☐☐☐
Strategy Takes the Risk Out of Achieving Success

The value and applicability of this exercise: The Theory *I* Table of Success Elements is at the center of producing our success. The more we learn to use it, the more successful we will become. The Theory *I* Exercise simulates the creation of a problem and offers us an opportunity to solve it using all of the tools of Theory *I*.

Problems crop up unpredictably, like a roll of the dice. These events can occur in the context of business or personal matters. To simulate the range of problems that can arise, we will actually roll dice to establish specific obstacles to obtaining success.

The first step in our exercise we randomly generate the five numbers to be filled in column 1 (in no particular order) after each class (GRIDS). In our example we produced and recorded the outcome of the dice as 2, 1, 4, 4, and 5 for GRIDS, respectively.

☐☐☐☐☐ THE THEORY *I* EXERCISE ☐☐☐☐☐
Strategy Takes the Risk Out of Achieving Success

SUCCESS STRATEGY	Part I: PROBLEM			Part II: SOLUTION			
Line	Situation and TSE			Table of Success Elements			Opportunity/Challenge Survey
Column→	1		2	3		4	5
Theory *I*	C	#	Element Name	C	#	Element Name	Single-Element Strategy
ROUND #1/#2/CASE							
1	G	2		G			
2	R	1		R			
3	I	4		I			
4	D	4		D			
5	S	5		S			

Next, we turn to The Table of Success Elements and record the corresponding element names. In our example we filled in *Agreement*, *Management*, Theory *M*, *Imagination*, and *Experiment*. For exercise purposes, if the G number and the R number happen to be the same, generate another number using the same technique until a different number results for either class.

☐☐☐☐☐ THE THEORY *I* EXERCISE ☐☐☐☐☐
Strategy Takes the Risk Out of Achieving Success

SUCCESS STRATEGY	Part I: PROBLEM			Part II: SOLUTION			
Line	Situation and TSE			Table of Success Elements			Opportunity/Challenge Survey
Column→	1		2	3		4	5
Theory *I*	C	#	Element Name	C	#	Element Name	Single-Element Strategy
	ROUND #1/#2/CASE						
1	G	2	*Agreement*	G			
2	R	1	*Management*	R			
3	I	4	Theory *M*	I			
4	D	4	*Imagination*	D			
5	S	5	*Experiment*	S			

At this point in the exercise we have produced a problem (Part I) that requires a solution (Part II). Many problems we face are the result of inappropriate combinations of *elements*. We notice that the rules of equivalent sets between Primary Goals and Basic Relationships have been broken (intentionally for exercise purposes). This creates a problem that requires a solution by either changing the Primary Goal to coincide with the Basic Relationship, or vice versa.

In our example we change the Basic Relationship as we complete columns 3 and 4 for lines 1 and 2. We continue lines 1 and 2 by completing the single-element strategy, referencing each class number to locate the corresponding single-element strategy within the Opportunity/Challenge Survey. After copying or paraphrasing these first two single-element strategies within their respective lines, we are now prepared to consider the most appropriate Principal Ideology.

❑❑❑❑❑ THE THEORY *I* EXERCISE ❑❑❑❑❑

Strategy Takes the Risk Out of Achieving Success

SUCCESS STRATEGY	Part I: PROBLEM				Part II: SOLUTION		
Line	Situation and TSE				Table of Success Elements		Opportunity/Challenge Survey
Column→	1		2	3	4		5
Theory *I*	C	#	Element Name	C	#	Element Name	Single-Element Strategy
ROUND #1/#2/CASE							
1	G	2	*Agreement*	G	2	*Agreement*	Discover rationale for differences, and work to **unify opinions** for mutual benefit.
2	R	1	*Management*	R	2	*Marketing*	Build acceptance of new ideas or concepts through thoroughness in personal **selling**.
3	I	4	Theory *M*	I			
4	D	4	*Imagination*	D			
5	S	5	*Experiment*	S			

The element names and single-element strategies provide guidance in ascertaining what set of assumptions would be sensible for communicating to others for gaining their support. In a **selling** environment, Theory I_Y is likely the most logical approach; although, through creative discussions we can create other scenarios where other Principal Ideologies may be more appropriate. In our example we combined portions from Theory Y and Theory I to produce a single-element strategy representing Theory I_Y to ensure understanding, friendly cooperation, and successful participation.

❑❑❑❑❑ THE THEORY *I* EXERCISE ❑❑❑❑❑
Strategy Takes the Risk Out of Achieving Success

SUCCESS STRATEGY	Part I: PROBLEM			Part II: SOLUTION			
Line	Situation and TSE			Table of Success Elements			Opportunity/Challenge Survey
Column→	1		2	3		4	5
Theory *I*	C	#	Element Name	C	#	Element Name	Single-Element Strategy
ROUND #1/#2/CASE							
1	G	2	*Agreement*	G	2	*Agreement*	Discover rationale for differences, and work to **unify opinions** for mutual benefit.
2	R	1	*Management*	R	2	*Marketing*	Build acceptance of new ideas or concepts through thoroughness in personal **selling**.
3	I	4	Theory *M*	I	5	**Theory I_Y**	Check **competencies** for comprehending ideas, and satisfy others via **camaraderie**.
4	D	4	*Imagination*	D			
5	S	5	*Experiment*	S			

Next, we need to consider the appropriate Prime Determinant for ensuring successful involvement of every key person. In our example we decided *imagination* was getting in the way of gaining *agreement*, and that we simply needed more *information*. When **selling** an idea, there may come a point in gaining *agreement* where more *information* rather than *imagination* is necessary to gain confidence for closing the *agreement*. Again, we completed the single-element strategy as before.

❑❑❑❑❑ THE THEORY *I* EXERCISE ❑❑❑❑❑
Strategy Takes the Risk Out of Achieving Success

SUCCESS STRATEGY	Part I: PROBLEM			Part II: SOLUTION		
Line	Situation and TSE			Table of Success Elements		Opportunity/Challenge Survey
Column→	1		2	3	4	5
Theory *I*	C	#	Element Name	C	#	Element Name	Single-Element Strategy
ROUND #1/#2/CASE						
1	G	2	*Agreement*	G	2	*Agreement*	Discover rationale for differences, and work to **unify opinions** for mutual benefit.
2	R	1	*Management*	R	2	*Marketing*	Build acceptance of new ideas or concepts through thoroughness in personal **selling**.
3	I	4	Theory *M*	I	5	Theory *I_Y*	Check **competencies** for comprehending ideas, and satisfy others via **camaraderie**.
4	D	4	*Imagination*	D	3	***Information***	Encourage learning of certain **facts/beliefs** to understand the requirements for success.
5	S	5	*Experiment*	S			

Finally, we must decide which Fundamental Step is appropriate within this particular situation. In our example we conclude that *experimenting* would not be most appropriate until there was a full understanding of all the *elements* impacting the situation. To be professional in attempting to gain *agreement*, taking the time to investigate the trade-offs of all the alternatives as revealed through a comprehensive **theory** provides excellent control for the one performing the **selling**. After referencing the single-element strategy from OCS, the collection of all classes of the single-element strategies comprises a full strategy.

◻◻◻◻◻ THE THEORY *I* EXERCISE ◻◻◻◻◻

Strategy Takes the Risk Out of Achieving Success

SUCCESS STRATEGY	Part I: PROBLEM				Part II: SOLUTION		
Line	Situation and TSE				Table of Success Elements		Opportunity/Challenge Survey
Column→	1	2		3	4		5
Theory *I*	C	#	Element Name	C	#	Element Name	Single-Element Strategy
	ROUND #1/#2/CASE						
1	G	2	*Agreement*	G	2	*Agreement*	Discover rationale for differences, and work to **unify opinions** for mutual benefit.
2	R	1	*Management*	R	2	*Marketing*	Build acceptance of new ideas or concepts through thoroughness in personal **selling**.
3	I	4	Theory *M*	I	5	Theory I_Y	Check **competencies** for comprehending ideas, and satisfy others via **camaraderie**.
4	D	4	*Imagination*	D	3	*Information*	Encourage learning of certain **facts/beliefs** to understand the requirements for success.
5	S	5	*Experiment*	S	3	*Elements*	Produce a complete picture of the road to success through a comprehensive **theory**.

By completing this exercise several times with an assumption that the problems/solutions are related, it is then possible to sequence these full strategies to create a superstrategy.

Case Study: Create an exercise by drawing upon your experiences, rather than the dice, to generate a PROBLEM. Your previous responses to the OCS statements/perspectives provide relevant input into your case study.

The following blank format is provided for your additional practice.

⬜⬜⬜⬜⬜ THE THEORY *I* EXERCISE ⬜⬜⬜⬜⬜
Strategy Takes the Risk Out of Achieving Success

SUCCESS STRATEGY	Part I: PROBLEM				Part II: SOLUTION	
Line	Situation and TSE			Table of Success Elements		Opportunity/Challenge Survey
Column→	1		2	3	4	5
Theory *I*	C	#	Element Name	C	#	Element Name	Single-Element Strategy
ROUND #1/#2/CASE						
1	G			G			
2	R			R			
3	I			I			
4	D			D			
5	S			S			

Summary and future value of this exercise: This exercise provides excellent perspectives for solving a wide variety of **challenges** and seeking the fulfillment of unlimited **opportunities**. The next time we wonder, "Why is the boss upset with me when the problem is not my fault?"; "Why is my client threatening to do business with competition after I made the best offer?"; "Why did my spouse change from a romantic partner to a bitter enemy?"; "Why do I want to give up when problems get way ahead of me?"; or "Why do expectations beyond my current abilities scare me?", we need to recognize there are alternatives that can favorably impact our motivation, development, and performance. By exploring the 1.55 times 10^{25} number of possibilities that could bring about such symptoms, we can create that many strategies to resolve them.

APPENDIX B - The Table of Success Elements with Arrows Exhibiting Rules of Theory *I*

MAPPING YOUR POTENTIAL TO SUCCESS

↓ Increasing Participation ←• Performance .... Balance .... Development →

	1	2	3	4	5
G oal — Primary Goals (Equivalent Sets)	*Accomplishment* G1	*Agreement* G2	*Affiliation* G3	*Affirmation* G4	*Achievement* G5
R elationship — Basic Relationships (Equivalent Sets)	*Management* R1	*Marketing* R2	*Matching* R3	*Ministry* R4	*Mastery* R5
I deology — Principal Ideologies (Subsets of Theory *I*)	Theory X — I1	Theory Y — I2	Theory Z — I3	Theory M — I4	Theory I ( ) — I5
D eterminant — Prime Determinants (Overlapping Sets)	*Instructions* D1	*Instincts* D2	*Information* D3	*Imagination* D4	*Individuality* D5
S tep — Fundamental Steps (Universal Sets)	*Environment* S1	*Experience* S2	*Elements* S3	*Exercises* S4	*Experiments* S5

The Table of Success Elements

© Corporate International Associates, Ltd.

The sample Opportunity/Challenge Surveys on the following pages address particular interests or roles of people. Select the OCS that applies most directly to your role, situation, or circumstances, and respond to it. With each OCS completed, you will be able to see the classifications and elements repeated. From this perspective you can focus specifically on recurring weaknesses while building strengths to aid in addressing future **opportunities** and **challenges**.

OPPORTUNITY/CHALLENGE SURVEY

SURVEY 1 - PROJECT LEADER: *Exploratory Tool for Producing Single-Element Strategies*

Keep a particular symptom of a problem in mind while considering statements and perspectives. Rank statements and perspectives by filling in solid circles covering "1" (disagree) through "5" (agree). Apply needed single-element strategies.

1 = totally disagree   2 = mostly disagree   3 = inconclusive   4 = mostly agree   5 = totally agree

C #	Successful Project Leader's Statements & Perspectives	Personal Ranking	Successful Project Leader's Single-Element Strategies
G1	Project participants perform all routine tasks at the expected/required level of proficiency.	1-2-3-4-5	Refine and perfect routine tasks to perform with **maximum effectiveness.**
G2	Project participants concur with project leader/client on what and how things need to be done.	1-2-3-4-5	Discover rationale for differences, and work to **unify opinions** for mutual benefit.
G3	Project participants/clients/management work closely together in support of the overall efforts.	1-2-3-4-5	Create a sincere partnership that results in **forming bonds** with the people involved.
G4	If work becomes overwhelming, project participants can get themselves back on track.	1-2-3-4-5	Assign appropriately sized tasks/responsibilities to encourage confidence and **confirm wholeness.**
G5	Project participants are developing new abilities to do what they need to do to ensure success.	1-2-3-4-5	Develop a new level of results by **ensuring growth.**
R1	Project leader enhances performances of participants by coordinating their joint efforts.	1-2-3-4-5	Have everyone perform what they do best to promote increased **synergism.**
R2	Discussions/suggestions provide valuable ideas supporting needs/desires of project participants.	1-2-3-4-5	Build acceptance of new ideas or concepts through thoroughness in personal **selling.**
R3	The strengths and weaknesses of project participants balance/complement each other.	1-2-3-4-5	Accommodate weaknesses with strengths through **sharing** of self.
R4	Project participants are not in need of support for self-assurance or personal direction.	1-2-3-4-5	Create confidence and self-assurance while **serving** other people's needs.
R5	Project participants are consistently developing their expertise for effectiveness in the project.	1-2-3-4-5	Develop critical **skills** to assure effectiveness for increasing individual qualifications.

154

I1	Project participants know what to do and how to do it without being told to perform.	1-2-3-4-5	Use clear **commands** to require all tasks to be performed properly.
I2	Project participants have the freedom to work at what is most meaningful and gratifying to them.	1-2-3-4-5	Encourage freedoms and satisfaction while working in an atmosphere of **camaraderie.**
I3	Project participants work cooperatively in support of one another as an effective team.	1-2-3-4-5	Bring working people together through overall **consensus.**
I4	When project participants feel job security, they still strive to improve their abilities/effectiveness.	1-2-3-4-5	Replace complacency with **confusion** requiring accountability and self-reliance for self-assurance.
I5	Project participants are being fulfilled while developing expertise to be most effective.	1-2-3-4-5	Develop self through new **competencies** in attaining personal and corporate results.
D1	Project participants are physically capable and mentally alert for performing work every day.	1-2-3-4-5	Ensure a strong performance by building upon **health directives.**
D2	Project participants sense a good probability that their efforts will produce success.	1-2-3-4-5	Encourage **natural tendencies** for seeking success by considering favorable options.
D3	Project participants know about the expected tasks and abilities needed to ensure project success.	1-2-3-4-5	Encourage learning of certain **facts/beliefs** to understand the requirements for success.
D4	Project participants see possibilities for quality/ productivity through increasing effectiveness.	1-2-3-4-5	Turn negative thinking and feelings into positive **hopes and dreams.**
D5	Project participants are developing their own sense of responsibility/control over success.	1-2-3-4-5	Encourage **self-determination** to develop personal fulfillment within corporate success.
S1	Project participants take the simplest route to increase chances for performance success.	1-2-3-4-5	Identify and evaluate **opportunities** for potential performance.
S2	Project participants feel a part of what needs to be done to create personal/corporate success.	1-2-3-4-5	Use **challenges** to create involvement and appreciation for what needs to be done.
S3	Project participants have a complete perspective on variables for overall corporate/personal success.	1-2-3-4-5	Produce a complete picture of the road to success through a comprehensive **theory.**
S4	Project participants are receiving the needed feedback/practice for fine-tuning their efforts.	1-2-3-4-5	To create critical proficiencies, incorporate new, meaningful ideas when practicing **activities.**
S5	Project participants are able to develop a total strategy for mapping their potential to success.	1-2-3-4-5	Develop orchestrated **to-do** lists for mapping each venture for success.

OPPORTUNITY/CHALLENGE SURVEY
SURVEY 2 - MANAGER: *Exploratory Tool for Producing Single-Element Strategies*

Keep a particular symptom of a problem in mind while considering statements and perspectives. Rank statements and perspectives by filling in solid circles covering "1" (disagree) through "5" (agree). Apply needed single-element strategies.

1 = totally disagree 2 = mostly disagree 3 = inconclusive 4 = mostly agree 5 = totally agree

C #	Successful Manager's Statements & Perspectives	Personal Ranking	Successful Manager's Single-Element Strategies
G1	Employees perform all routine tasks at the expected/required level of proficiency.	1-2-3-4-5	Refine and perfect routine tasks to perform with **maximum effectiveness.**
G2	Employees concur with management/colleagues/clients on what and how things need to be done.	1-2-3-4-5	Discover rationale for differences, and work to **unify opinions** for mutual benefit.
G3	Employees/clients/management work closely together while supporting their overall efforts.	1-2-3-4-5	Create a sincere partnership that results in **forming bonds** with the people involved.
G4	If work becomes overwhelming, employees can get themselves back on track.	1-2-3-4-5	Assign appropriately sized tasks/responsibilities to encourage confidence and **confirm wholeness.**
G5	Employees are developing new abilities to do what they need to do to ensure success.	1-2-3-4-5	Develop a new level of results by **ensuring growth.**
R1	Employees make joint personal efforts to coordinate ways to enhance efforts.	1-2-3-4-5	Have everyone perform what they do best to promote increased **synergism.**
R2	Discussions/suggestions provide valuable ideas employees find supportive of their needs/desires.	1-2-3-4-5	Build acceptance of new ideas or concepts through thoroughness in personal **selling.**
R3	The strengths and weaknesses of employees balance and complement each other.	1-2-3-4-5	Accommodate weaknesses with strengths through **sharing** of self.
R4	Employees are not in need of support for self-assurance or personal direction.	1-2-3-4-5	Create confidence and self-assurance while **serving** other people's needs.
R5	Employees are consistently developing expertise in learning (and effectively practicing) their work.	1-2-3-4-5	Develop critical **skills** to assure effectiveness for increasing individual qualifications.

I1	Employees know what to do, how to do it, and they respond without being told to perform.	1-2-3-4-5	Use clear **commands** to require all tasks to be performed properly.
I2	Employees have the freedom to work at what is most meaningful and gratifying to them.	1-2-3-4-5	Encourage freedoms and satisfaction while working in an atmosphere of **camaraderie**.
I3	Employees work cooperatively in support of one another as an effective team.	1-2-3-4-5	Bring working people together through overall **consensus**.
I4	When employees feel job security, they still strive to increase knowledge and effectiveness.	1-2-3-4-5	Replace complacency with **confusion** requiring accountability and self-reliance for self-assurance.
I5	Employees are being fulfilled while developing expertise to be most effective in their work.	1-2-3-4-5	Develop self through new **competencies** in attaining personal and corporate results.
D1	Employees are physically capable and mentally alert for performing their work every day.	1-2-3-4-5	Ensure a strong performance by building upon **health directives**.
D2	Employees sense a good probability that their efforts will produce success.	1-2-3-4-5	Encourage **natural tendencies** for seeking success by considering favorable options.
D3	Employees know enough about expected tasks/abilities needed to ensure personal/corporate success.	1-2-3-4-5	Encourage learning of certain **facts/beliefs** to understand the requirements for success.
D4	Employees see possibilities for productivity/quality results through increasing effectiveness.	1-2-3-4-5	Turn negative thinking and feelings into positive **hopes and dreams**.
D5	Employees are capable of developing their own sense of responsibility/control over success.	1-2-3-4-5	Encourage **self-determination** to develop personal fulfillment within corporate success.
S1	Employees take the simplest route first, to increase chances for performance success.	1-2-3-4-5	Identify and evaluate **opportunities** for potential performance.
S2	Employees feel a part of what needs to be done for creating personal and corporate success.	1-2-3-4-5	Use **challenges** to create involvement and appreciation for what needs to be done.
S3	Employees have a complete perspective on variables impacting corporate and personal success.	1-2-3-4-5	Produce a complete picture of the road to success through a comprehensive **theory**.
S4	Employees are receiving needed feedback/practice for fine-tuning and improving their work efforts.	1-2-3-4-5	To create critical proficiencies, incorporate new, meaningful ideas when practicing **activities**.
S5	Employees are able to develop a total strategy for mapping their potential to success.	1-2-3-4-5	Develop orchestrated **to-do** lists for mapping each venture for success.

OPPORTUNITY/CHALLENGE SURVEY

SURVEY 3 - EMPLOYEE: *Exploratory Tool for Producing Single-Element Strategies*

Keep a particular symptom of a problem in mind while considering statements and perspectives. Rank statements and perspectives by filling in solid circles covering "1" (disagree) through "5" (agree). Apply needed single-element strategies.

1 = totally disagree   2 = mostly disagree   3 = inconclusive   4 = mostly agree   5 = totally agree

C#	Successful Employee's Statements & Perspectives	Personal Ranking	Successful Employee's Single-Element Strategies
G1	I perform all routine tasks at the expected/required level of proficiency.	1-2-3-4-5	Refine and perfect routine tasks to perform with **maximum effectiveness**.
G2	I concur with colleagues/management/clients on what and how things need to be done.	1-2-3-4-5	Discover rationale for differences, and work to **unify opinions** for mutual benefit.
G3	I work closely together with clients/management/colleagues while supporting our overall efforts.	1-2-3-4-5	Create a sincere partnership that results in **forming bonds** with the people involved.
G4	If work becomes overwhelming, I can get myself back on track.	1-2-3-4-5	Assign appropriately sized tasks/responsibilities to encourage confidence and **confirm wholeness**.
G5	I am developing new abilities to do what I need to do to ensure success.	1-2-3-4-5	Develop a new level of results by **ensuring growth**.
R1	I make joint personal efforts to coordinate ways to enhance performances.	1-2-3-4-5	Have everyone perform what they do best to promote increased **synergism**.
R2	Discussions or suggestions provide ideas I find valuable for satisfying working needs/desires.	1-2-3-4-5	Build acceptance of new ideas or concepts through thoroughness in personal **selling**.
R3	My strengths and weaknesses are in balance with other employees, and we complement each other.	1-2-3-4-5	Accommodate weaknesses with strengths through **sharing** of self.
R4	I am not in need of support for self-assurance or personal direction.	1-2-3-4-5	Create confidence and self-assurance while **serving** other people's needs.
R5	I am consistently developing my expertise in learning (and effectively practicing) my work.	1-2-3-4-5	Develop critical **skills** to assure effectiveness for increasing individual qualifications.

	Statement	Scale	Directive
I1	In my job I know what to do, how to do it, and I respond without being told to perform.	1-2-3-4-5	Use clear **commands** to require all tasks to be performed properly.
I2	I have the freedom to work at what is most meaningful and gratifying to me.	1-2-3-4-5	Encourage freedoms and satisfaction while working in an atmosphere of **camaraderie.**
I3	I work cooperatively in support of my fellow workers as an effective team.	1-2-3-4-5	Bring working people together through overall **consensus.**
I4	When I feel job security at work, I still strive to improve my knowledge/abilities/effectiveness.	1-2-3-4-5	Replace complacency with **confusion** requiring accountability and self-reliance for self-assurance.
I5	I am being fulfilled while developing expertise to be most effective in my work.	1-2-3-4-5	Develop self through new **competencies** in attaining personal and corporate results.
D1	I am physically capable and mentally alert for performing my job every day.	1-2-3-4-5	Ensure a strong performance by building upon **health directives.**
D2	I sense a good probability that my efforts will produce success.	1-2-3-4-5	Encourage **natural tendencies** for seeking success by considering favorable options.
D3	I know enough about the expected tasks/abilities needed to ensure personal and corporate success.	1-2-3-4-5	Encourage learning of certain **facts/beliefs** to understand the requirements for success.
D4	I see possibilities for increasing my overall effectiveness for greater productivity and quality.	1-2-3-4-5	Turn negative thinking and feelings into positive **hopes and dreams.**
D5	I am capable of developing my own sense of responsibility and control over my success.	1-2-3-4-5	Encourage **self-determination** to develop personal fulfillment within corporate success.
S1	I take the simplest route first, to increase chances for my work performance success.	1-2-3-4-5	Identify and evaluate **opportunities** for potential performance.
S2	I feel a part of what needs to be done for creating personal and corporate success.	1-2-3-4-5	Use **challenges** to create involvement and appreciation for what needs to be done.
S3	I have a complete perspective on variables contributing to total corporate and personal success.	1-2-3-4-5	Produce a complete picture of the road to success through a comprehensive **theory.**
S4	I am receiving needed feedback and practice for fine-tuning and improving my working efforts.	1-2-3-4-5	To create critical proficiencies, incorporate new, meaningful ideas when practicing **activities.**
S5	I am able to develop a total strategy for mapping my personal and corporate potential to success.	1-2-3-4-5	Develop orchestrated **to-do** lists for mapping each venture for success.

159

OPPORTUNITY/CHALLENGE SURVEY
SURVEY 4 - SALESPERSON: *Exploratory Tool for Producing Single-Element Strategies*

Keep a particular symptom of a problem in mind while considering statements and perspectives. Rank statements and perspectives by filling in solid circles covering "1" (disagree) through "5" (agree). Apply needed single-element strategies.

1 = totally disagree   2 = mostly disagree   3 = inconclusive   4 = mostly agree   5 = totally agree

C #	Successful Salesperson's Statements & Perspectives	Personal Ranking	Successful Salesperson's Single-Element Strategies
G1	I perform all routine selling tasks at the expected/required level of proficiency.	1-2-3-4-5	Refine and perfect routine tasks to perform with **maximum effectiveness.**
G2	I concur with clients/colleagues/management on what and how things need to be done.	1-2-3-4-5	Discover rationale for differences, and work to **unify opinions** for mutual benefit.
G3	I, my client, and my sales team work closely together while supporting our overall efforts.	1-2-3-4-5	Create a sincere partnership that results in **forming bonds** with the people involved.
G4	If work becomes overwhelming, I can get myself back on track.	1-2-3-4-5	Assign appropriately sized tasks/responsibilities to encourage confidence and **confirm wholeness.**
G5	I am developing new selling abilities to do what I need to do to reach top sales results.	1-2-3-4-5	Develop a new level of results by **ensuring growth.**
R1	I make joint personal efforts to coordinate ways to enhance sales performance.	1-2-3-4-5	Have everyone perform what they do best to promote increased **synergism.**
R2	Discussions or suggestions provide ideas I find valuable for satisfying my client's needs/desires.	1-2-3-4-5	Build acceptance of new ideas or concepts through thoroughness in personal **selling**.
R3	The strengths and weaknesses of the sales team/client balance and complement each other.	1-2-3-4-5	Accommodate weaknesses with strengths through **sharing** of self.
R4	I am not in need of support for self-assurance or personal direction.	1-2-3-4-5	Create confidence and self-assurance while **serving** other people's needs.
R5	I am consistently developing my expertise in learning (and effectively practicing) how to sell.	1-2-3-4-5	Develop critical **skills** to assure effectiveness for increasing individual qualifications.

160

Code	Statement	Scale	
I1	In selling, I know what to do, how to do it, and I respond without being told to perform.	1-2-3-4-5	Use clear **commands** to require all tasks to be performed properly.
I2	I have the freedom to work at what is most meaningful and gratifying to me in selling.	1-2-3-4-5	Encourage freedoms and satisfaction while working in an atmosphere of **camaraderie**.
I3	My fellow workers work cooperatively in support of one another as an effective sales team.	1-2-3-4-5	Bring working people together through overall **consensus**.
I4	When I feel secure with my sales results, I still strive to increase my selling effectiveness.	1-2-3-4-5	Replace complacency with **confusion** requiring accountability and self-reliance for self-assurance.
I5	I am being fulfilled while developing expertise to be most effective in increasing my overall sales.	1-2-3-4-5	Develop self through new **competencies** in attaining personal and corporate results.
D1	I am physically capable and mentally alert for performing as a sales representative every day.	1-2-3-4-5	Ensure a strong performance by building upon **health directives**.
D2	I sense a good probability that my selling efforts will produce success.	1-2-3-4-5	Encourage **natural tendencies** for seeking success by considering favorable options.
D3	I know enough about expected selling tasks/abilities needed to ensure personal/corporate success.	1-2-3-4-5	Encourage learning of certain **facts/beliefs** to understand the requirements for success.
D4	I see possibilities for how to increase sales that will exceed all of my previous sales records.	1-2-3-4-5	Turn negative thinking and feelings into positive **hopes and dreams**.
D5	I am capable of developing my own sense of responsibility and control over selling success.	1-2-3-4-5	Encourage **self-determination** to develop personal fulfillment within corporate success.
S1	I take the simplest route first, to increase chances for successful sales performances.	1-2-3-4-5	Identify and evaluate **opportunities** for potential performance.
S2	I personally feel a part of what needs to be done to create selling success.	1-2-3-4-5	Use **challenges** to create involvement and appreciation for what needs to be done.
S3	I have a complete perspective on variables impacting/producing selling success.	1-2-3-4-5	Produce a complete picture of the road to success through a comprehensive **theory**.
S4	I am receiving needed feedback and practice for fine-tuning and improving my selling efforts.	1-2-3-4-5	To create critical proficiencies, incorporate new, meaningful ideas when practicing **activities**.
S5	I am able to develop a total strategy for mapping my potential for sales to my sales success.	1-2-3-4-5	Develop orchestrated **to-do** lists for mapping each venture for success.

OPPORTUNITY/CHALLENGE SURVEY
SURVEY 5 - JOB SEEKER: *Exploratory Tool for Producing Single-Element Strategies*

Keep a particular symptom of a problem in mind while considering statements and perspectives. Rank statements and perspectives by filling in solid circles covering "1" (disagree) through "5" (agree). Apply needed single-element strategies.

1 = totally disagree   2 = mostly disagree   3 = inconclusive   4 = mostly agree   5 = totally agree

C #	Successful Job Seeker's Statements & Perspectives	Personal Ranking	Successful Job Seeker's Single-Element Strategies
G1	I perform all routine job-seeking tasks at the expected/required level of proficiency.	1-2-3-4-5	Refine and perfect routine tasks to perform with **maximum effectiveness.**
G2	I concur with job interviewers/successful people in my field on what/how things need to be done.	1-2-3-4-5	Discover rationale for differences, and work to **unify opinions** for mutual benefit.
G3	I work closely together with people who can offer me ideas/support for finding a meaningful job.	1-2-3-4-5	Create a sincere partnership that results in **forming bonds** with the people involved.
G4	If finding a job becomes overwhelming, I can get myself back on track.	1-2-3-4-5	Assign appropriately sized tasks/responsibilities to encourage confidence and **confirm wholeness.**
G5	I am developing new abilities to do what I need to do to meet new job requirements/demands.	1-2-3-4-5	Develop a new level of results by **ensuring growth.**
R1	I make joint personal efforts to coordinate ways to enhance job-seeking efforts.	1-2-3-4-5	Have everyone perform what they do best to promote increased **synergism.**
R2	Discussions or suggestions provide ideas I find valuable in satisfying job-seeking needs/desires.	1-2-3-4-5	Build acceptance of new ideas or concepts through thoroughness in personal **selling.**
R3	My strengths/weaknesses are a good balance to meet/complement my job-seeking requirements.	1-2-3-4-5	Accommodate weaknesses with strengths through **sharing** of self.
R4	I do not need support for self-assurance or personal direction while seeking a new job.	1-2-3-4-5	Create confidence and self-assurance while **serving** other people's needs.
R5	I am consistently developing my expertise in learning (and effectively practicing) job-seeking capabilities.	1-2-3-4-5	Develop critical **skills** to assure effectiveness for increasing individual qualifications.

162

	Statement	Rating	Description
I1	In job finding, I know what to do, how to do it, and I respond without being told to perform.	1-2-3-4-5	Use clear **commands** to require all tasks to be performed properly.
I2	In seeking a job, I have the freedom to explore work that is meaningful and gratifying to me.	1-2-3-4-5	Encourage freedoms and satisfaction while working in an atmosphere of **camaraderie.**
I3	I work cooperatively with anyone who can assist me in becoming successfully employed.	1-2-3-4-5	Bring working people together through overall **consensus.**
I4	When I feel secure seeking a job, I still strive to increase my knowledge, skill, and effectiveness.	1-2-3-4-5	Replace complacency with **confusion** requiring accountability and self-reliance for self-assurance.
I5	When I seek employment, I see new ways to produce personal fulfillment/corporate success.	1-2-3-4-5	Develop self through new **competencies** in attaining personal and corporate results.
D1	I am physically capable and mentally alert for performing a job search as a full-time job.	1-2-3-4-5	Ensure a strong performance by building upon **health directives.**
D2	I sense a good probability that my job-seeking efforts will produce success.	1-2-3-4-5	Encourage **natural tendencies** for seeking success by considering favorable options.
D3	I know enough about the expected tasks/abilities needed to ensure success in finding a desirable job.	1-2-3-4-5	Encourage learning of certain **facts/beliefs** to understand the requirements for success.
D4	I see possibilities for finding a new job that could create considerable success.	1-2-3-4-5	Turn negative thinking and feelings into positive **hopes and dreams.**
D5	I am capable of developing my own sense of responsibility and control over getting a job.	1-2-3-4-5	Encourage **self-determination** to develop personal fulfillment within corporate success.
S1	I take the simplest route first, to increase chances for finding a meaningful job.	1-2-3-4-5	Identify and evaluate **opportunities** for potential performance.
S2	I feel a part of what needs to be done for creating or attracting good job offerings.	1-2-3-4-5	Use **challenges** to create involvement and appreciation for what needs to be done.
S3	I have a complete perspective on variables for generating a productive job search.	1-2-3-4-5	Produce a complete picture of the road to success through a comprehensive **theory.**
S4	I am receiving needed feedback and practice for fine-tuning/improving my job-finding abilities.	1-2-3-4-5	To create critical proficiencies, incorporate new, meaningful ideas when practicing **activities.**
S5	I am able to develop a strategy for mapping my potential for finding/creating a job.	1-2-3-4-5	Develop orchestrated **to-do** lists for mapping each venture for success.

163

OPPORTUNITY/CHALLENGE SURVEY

SURVEY 6 - STUDENT: *Exploratory Tool for Producing Single-Element Strategies*

Keep a particular symptom of a problem in mind while considering statements and perspectives. Rank statements and perspectives by filling in solid circles covering "1" (disagree) through "5" (agree). Apply needed single-element strategies.

1 = totally disagree   2 = mostly disagree   3 = inconclusive   4 = mostly agree   5 = totally agree

C #	Successful Student's Statements & Perspectives	Personal Ranking	Successful Student's Single-Element Strategies
G1	I perform all routine academic tasks at the expected/required level of proficiency.	1-2-3-4-5	Refine and perfect routine tasks to perform with **maximum effectiveness.**
G2	I concur with colleagues and teachers on what and how things need to be done.	1-2-3-4-5	Discover rationale for differences, and work to **unify opinions** for mutual benefit.
G3	I am working closely together with other students while supporting my team's efforts.	1-2-3-4-5	Create a sincere partnership that results in **forming bonds** with the people involved.
G4	If my studies become overwhelming, I can get myself back on track.	1-2-3-4-5	Assign appropriately sized tasks/responsibilities to encourage confidence and **confirm wholeness.**
G5	I am developing new abilities to do what I need to do to meet academic demands.	1-2-3-4-5	Develop a new level of results by **ensuring growth.**
R1	I make joint personal efforts to coordinate ways to enhance academic efforts.	1-2-3-4-5	Have everyone perform what they do best to promote increased **synergism.**
R2	Discussions or suggestions provide ideas I find valuable for satisfying academic needs/desires.	1-2-3-4-5	Build acceptance of new ideas or concepts through thoroughness in personal **selling.**
R3	My strengths/weaknesses are a good balance to meet/ complement my study team's efforts/requirements.	1-2-3-4-5	Accommodate weaknesses with strengths through **sharing** of self.
R4	I am not in need of support for self-assurance or personal direction.	1-2-3-4-5	Create confidence and self-assurance while **serving** other people's needs.
R5	I am consistently developing my expertise in learning (and effectively practicing) how to apply knowledge.	1-2-3-4-5	Develop critical **skills** to assure effectiveness for increasing individual qualifications.

164

I1	In academics, I know what to do, how to do it, and I respond without being told to perform.	1-2-3-4-5	Use clear **commands** to require all tasks to be performed properly.
I2	As a student I have freedom to do what is most meaningful/gratifying to assure my success.	1-2-3-4-5	Encourage freedoms and satisfaction while working in an atmosphere of **camaraderie**.
I3	My fellow students and I work cooperatively in support of one another as an effective team.	1-2-3-4-5	Bring working people together through overall **consensus**.
I4	When I feel secure in my subjects, I still strive to increase my knowledge, skill, and effectiveness.	1-2-3-4-5	Replace complacency with **confusion** requiring accountability and self-reliance for self-assurance.
I5	Through my academic efforts I am being fulfilled while developing expertise to be most effective.	1-2-3-4-5	Develop self through new **competencies** in attaining personal and academic results.
D1	I remain physically capable and mentally alert to offer my best efforts for academic performance.	1-2-3-4-5	Ensure a strong performance by building upon **health directives**.
D2	I sense good probabilities my study efforts will produce scholastic/career success.	1-2-3-4-5	Encourage **natural tendencies** for seeking success by considering favorable options.
D3	I know enough about the expected tasks/abilities needed to ensure a good scholastic standing.	1-2-3-4-5	Encourage learning of certain **facts/beliefs** to understand the requirements for success.
D4	I can see possibilities for scholastic success that exceeds all of my previous attainments.	1-2-3-4-5	Turn negative thinking and feelings into positive **hopes and dreams**.
D5	I am capable of developing my own sense of responsibility/control over academic success.	1-2-3-4-5	Encourage **self-determination** to develop personal fulfillment within academic success.
S1	I can take the simplest performance route first, to increase chances of academic success.	1-2-3-4-5	Identify and evaluate **opportunities** for potential performance.
S2	I feel a part of what needs to be done for creating my academic success.	1-2-3-4-5	Use **challenges** to create involvement and appreciation for what needs to be done.
S3	I have a complete perspective on variables for producing academic success.	1-2-3-4-5	Produce a complete picture of the road to success through a comprehensive **theory**.
S4	I am receiving needed feedback and practice for fine-tuning and improving my academic efforts.	1-2-3-4-5	To create critical proficiencies, incorporate new, meaningful ideas when practicing **activities**.
S5	I am able to develop a total strategy for mapping my academic potential to my academic success.	1-2-3-4-5	Develop orchestrated **to-do** lists for mapping each venture for success.

OPPORTUNITY/CHALLENGE SURVEY
SURVEY 7 – ATHLETE: *Exploratory Tool for Producing Single-Element Strategies*

Keep a particular symptom of a problem in mind while considering statements and perspectives. Rank statements and perspectives by filling in solid circles covering "1" (disagree) through "5" (agree). Apply needed single-element strategies.

1 = totally disagree   2 = mostly disagree   3 = inconclusive   4 = mostly agree   5 = totally agree

C #	Successful Athlete's Statements & Perspectives	Personal Ranking	Successful Athlete's Single-Element Strategies
G1	I perform all routine moves/techniques at the expected/required level of proficiency.	1-2-3-4-5	Refine and perfect routine tasks to perform with **maximum effectiveness.**
G2	I concur with colleagues and coaches on what and how things need to be done.	1-2-3-4-5	Discover rationale for differences, and work to **unify opinions** for mutual benefit.
G3	I am working closely together with other athletes while supporting the team's overall efforts.	1-2-3-4-5	Create a sincere partnership that results in **forming bonds** with the people involved.
G4	If the demands of my sport become overwhelming, I can get myself back on track.	1-2-3-4-5	Assign appropriately sized tasks/responsibilities to encourage confidence and **confirm wholeness.**
G5	I am developing new abilities to do what I need to do to meet my athletic demands or endeavors.	1-2-3-4-5	Develop a new level of results by **ensuring growth.**
R1	I make joint personal efforts to coordinate ways to enhance team performances.	1-2-3-4-5	Have everyone perform what they do best to promote increased **synergism.**
R2	Discussions or suggestions provide ideas I find valuable for satisfying my athletic needs/desires.	1-2-3-4-5	Build acceptance of new ideas or concepts through thoroughness in personal **selling.**
R3	My strengths/weaknesses are a good balance to meet/complement our team's efforts/requirements.	1-2-3-4-5	Accommodate weaknesses with strengths through **sharing** of self.
R4	I am not in need of support for self-assurance or personal direction.	1-2-3-4-5	Create confidence and self-assurance while **serving** other people's needs.
R5	I am consistently developing my expertise in learning (and effectively practicing) my sport.	1-2-3-4-5	Develop critical **skills** to assure effectiveness for increasing individual qualifications.

I1	In this sport, I know what to do, how to do it, and I respond without being told to perform.	1-2-3-4-5	Use clear **commands** to require all tasks to be performed properly.
I2	As an athlete I have the freedom to do what is most meaningful and gratifying to me.	1-2-3-4-5	Encourage freedoms and satisfaction while working in an atmosphere of **camaraderie**.
I3	My fellow athletes and I work cooperatively in support of one another as an effective team.	1-2-3-4-5	Bring working people together through overall **consensus**.
I4	When I feel secure in my sport, I still strive to increase my knowledge, skill, and effectiveness.	1-2-3-4-5	Replace complacency with **confusion** requiring accountability and self-reliance for self-assurance.
I5	Through athletic endeavors, I am being fulfilled while developing expertise to be most effective.	1-2-3-4-5	Develop self through new **competencies** in attaining personal and team results.
D1	I remain physically capable and mentally alert to offer my best efforts for athletic performance.	1-2-3-4-5	Ensure a strong performance by building upon **health directives**.
D2	I sense a good probability that my workout efforts will produce athletic success.	1-2-3-4-5	Encourage **natural tendencies** for seeking success by considering favorable options.
D3	I know enough about the expected tasks/abilities needed to ensure my athletic success.	1-2-3-4-5	Encourage learning of certain **facts/beliefs** to understand the requirements for success.
D4	I see possibilities for athletic success that exceed all of my previous sports attainments.	1-2-3-4-5	Turn negative thinking and feelings into positive **hopes and dreams**.
D5	I am capable of developing my own sense of responsibility/control over athletic success.	1-2-3-4-5	Encourage **self-determination** to develop personal fulfillment within team success.
S1	I take the simplest performance route first, to increase chances of my athletic success.	1-2-3-4-5	Identify and evaluate **opportunities** for potential performance.
S2	I feel a part of what needs to be done for creating athletic success.	1-2-3-4-5	Use **challenges** to create involvement and appreciation for what needs to be done.
S3	I have a complete perspective on variables for producing athletic success.	1-2-3-4-5	Produce a complete picture of the road to success through a comprehensive **theory**.
S4	I am receiving needed feedback and practice for fine-tuning and improving my athletic success.	1-2-3-4-5	To create critical proficiencies, incorporate new, meaningful ideas when practicing **activities**.
S5	I am able to develop a total strategy for mapping my athletic potential to my athletic success.	1-2-3-4-5	Develop orchestrated **to-do** lists for mapping each venture for success.

OPPORTUNITY/CHALLENGE SURVEY

SURVEY 8 - SPOUSE: *Exploratory Tool for Producing Single-Element Strategies*

Keep a particular symptom of a problem in mind while considering statements and perspectives. Rank statements and perspectives by filling in solid circles covering "1" (disagree) through "5" (agree). Apply needed single-element strategies.

1 = totally disagree   2 = mostly disagree   3 = inconclusive   4 = mostly agree   5 = totally agree

C #	Successful Spouse's Statements & Perspectives	Personal Ranking	Successful Spouse's Single-Element Strategies
G1	My spouse and I perform all routine marital responsibilities at the expected level of proficiency.	1-2-3-4-5	Refine and perfect routine tasks to perform with **maximum effectiveness.**
G2	My spouse and I concur on what and how things need to be done.	1-2-3-4-5	Discover rationale for differences, and work to **unify opinions** for mutual benefit.
G3	My spouse and I are working closely together while supporting overall joint efforts.	1-2-3-4-5	Create a sincere partnership that results in **forming bonds** with the people involved.
G4	If difficulties in my marriage become overwhelming, my spouse and I can get ourselves back on track.	1-2-3-4-5	Assign appropriately sized tasks/responsibilities to encourage confidence and **confirm wholeness.**
G5	I am developing new abilities to do what I need to do to meet all marital requirements/needs.	1-2-3-4-5	Develop a new level of results by **ensuring growth.**
R1	I make joint personal efforts to coordinate ways to enhance spouse partnership.	1-2-3-4-5	Have everyone perform what they do best to promote increased **synergism.**
R2	Discussions or suggestions provide ideas I find valuable for meeting my marital desires/expectations.	1-2-3-4-5	Build acceptance of new ideas or concepts through thoroughness in personal **selling.**
R3	Our strengths/weaknesses are a good balance to meet/complement our marriage/personal requirements.	1-2-3-4-5	Accommodate weaknesses with strengths through **sharing** of self.
R4	I and my spouse are not in need of support for self-assurance or personal direction.	1-2-3-4-5	Create confidence and self-assurance while **serving** other people's needs.
R5	My spouse and I are consistently developing expertise/effectiveness in relating to each other.	1-2-3-4-5	Develop critical **skills** to assure effectiveness for increasing individual qualifications.

I1	In marriage, I know what to do, how to do it, and I respond without being told to perform.	1-2-3-4-5	Use clear **commands** to require all tasks to be performed properly.
I2	My spouse and I have the freedom to do what is most meaningful and gratifying to us personally.	1-2-3-4-5	Encourage freedoms and satisfaction while working in an atmosphere of **camaraderie.**
I3	My spouse and I work cooperatively together in support of one another as an effective team.	1-2-3-4-5	Bring working people together through overall **consensus.**
I4	When I feel secure in my marriage, I still strive to increase my love/knowledge/effectiveness.	1-2-3-4-5	Replace complacency with **confusion** requiring accountability and self-reliance for self-assurance.
I5	Through my marriage I am being fulfilled while developing expertise to increase effectiveness.	1-2-3-4-5	Develop self through new **competencies** in attaining personal and joint results.
D1	I am physically capable and mentally alert for enjoying time together with my spouse.	1-2-3-4-5	Ensure a strong performance by building upon **health directives.**
D2	I sense a good probability that my love will ultimately ensure marital happiness/fulfillment.	1-2-3-4-5	Encourage **natural tendencies** for seeking success by considering favorable options.
D3	I know enough about the expected tasks/abilities needed for marriage to ensure my success.	1-2-3-4-5	Encourage learning of certain **facts/beliefs** to understand the requirements for success.
D4	I can see possibilities for my spouse and me to progressively improve and find joy in our marriage.	1-2-3-4-5	Turn negative thinking and feelings into positive **hopes and dreams.**
D5	I am capable of developing my own sense of responsibility/control over marital success.	1-2-3-4-5	Encourage **self-determination** to develop personal fulfillment within a successful marriage.
S1	I take the simplest performance route first, to increase chances of marital happiness.	1-2-3-4-5	Identify and evaluate **opportunities** for potential performance.
S2	I feel a part of what needs to be done for creating marital success.	1-2-3-4-5	Use **challenges** to create involvement and appreciation for what needs to be done.
S3	I have a complete perspective on variables for producing marital happiness.	1-2-3-4-5	Produce a complete picture of the road to success through a comprehensive **theory.**
S4	I am receiving needed feedback for fine-tuning and improving my marital happiness/success.	1-2-3-4-5	To create critical proficiencies, incorporate new, meaningful ideas when practicing **activities.**
S5	I am able to develop a total strategy for mapping my potential for happiness to marriage success.	1-2-3-4-5	Develop orchestrated **to-do** lists for mapping each venture for success.

OPPORTUNITY/CHALLENGE SURVEY

SURVEY 9 - _____ : Exploratory Tool for Producing Single-Element Strategies

Keep a particular symptom of a problem in mind while considering statements and perspectives. Rank statements and perspectives by filling in solid circles covering "1" (disagree) through "5" (agree). Apply needed single-element strategies.

1 = totally disagree   2 = mostly disagree   3 = inconclusive   4 = mostly agree   5 = totally agree

C #	Successful _____ Person's Statements & Perspectives	Personal Ranking	Successful _____ Person's Single-Element Strategies
G1		1-2-3-4-5	Refine and perfect routine tasks to perform with **maximum effectiveness.**
G2		1-2-3-4-5	Discover rationale for differences, and work to **unify opinions** for mutual benefit.
G3		1-2-3-4-5	Create a sincere partnership that results in **forming bonds** with the people involved.
G4		1-2-3-4-5	Assign appropriately sized tasks/responsibilities to encourage confidence and **confirm wholeness.**
G5		1-2-3-4-5	Develop a new level of results by **ensuring growth.**
R1		1-2-3-4-5	Have everyone perform what they do best to promote increased **synergism.**
R2		1-2-3-4-5	Build acceptance of new ideas or concepts through thoroughness in personal **selling.**
R3		1-2-3-4-5	Accommodate weaknesses with strengths through **sharing** of self.
R4		1-2-3-4-5	Create confidence and self-assurance while **serving** other people's needs.
R5		1-2-3-4-5	Develop critical **skills** to assure effectiveness for increasing individual qualifications.

170

I1	1-2-3-4-5	Use clear **commands** to require all tasks to be performed properly.
I2	1-2-3-4-5	Encourage freedoms and satisfaction while working in an atmosphere of **camaraderie.**
I3	1-2-3-4-5	Bring working people together through overall **consensus.**
I4	1-2-3-4-5	Replace complacency with **confusion** requiring accountability and self-reliance for self-assurance.
I5	1-2-3-4-5	Develop self through new **competencies** in attaining personal and corporate results.
D1	1-2-3-4-5	Ensure a strong performance by building upon **health directives.**
D2	1-2-3-4-5	Encourage **natural tendencies** for seeking success by considering favorable options.
D3	1-2-3-4-5	Encourage learning of certain **facts/beliefs** to understand the requirements for success.
D4	1-2-3-4-5	Turn negative thinking and feelings into positive **hopes and dreams.**
D5	1-2-3-4-5	Encourage **self-determination** to develop personal fulfillment within corporate success.
S1	1-2-3-4-5	Identify and evaluate **opportunities** for potential performance.
S2	1-2-3-4-5	Use **challenges** to create involvement and appreciation for what needs to be done.
S3	1-2-3-4-5	Produce a complete picture of the road to success through a comprehensive **theory.**
S4	1-2-3-4-5	To create critical proficiencies, incorporate new, meaningful ideas when practicing **activities.**
S5	1-2-3-4-5	Develop orchestrated **to-do** lists for mapping each venture for success.

171

GLOSSARY

Accomplishment. The performance of routine tasks at the expected or required level of proficiency. See G1 in the Table of Success Elements.

Achievement. The development of new skills and abilities to do what needs to be done. See G5 in the Table of Success Elements.

Affiliation. The cooperative efforts that support joint endeavors. See G3 in the Table of Success Elements.

Affirmation. The support given to an individual in order to ease burdens, build confidence, and meet personal needs. See G4 in the Table of Success Elements.

Agreement. Concurrence on what and how things should be done. See G2 in the Table of Success Elements.

Attributes. Attributes are the descriptive words below each element in the Table of Success Elements. They specify the foundation and form of the element. Focusing on an attribute leads to the development of that element. Attributes control the development of elements and impact the formation of strategies.

Class (of *Elements*). Elements are grouped into five classes: Goals, Relationships, Ideologies, Determinants, and Steps (GRIDS). The five classes are governed by the specific rules of set theory.

Disappointment. The difference between high expectations and low performance.

Dogma. An all-encompassing presumed fact from a self-proclaimed authority who assumes omnipotence in a particular subject area.

Element. The smallest, unique distinction of a force, factor, or focus that will impact the result. The elements of Theory *I* are what impacts what we have done, can do, or will do. Elements are used to raise questions that define root problems, cutting through superficial symptoms. Elements belong to one of the five major areas or classes of elements: Goals, Relationships, Ideologies, Determinants, and Steps, referred to as GRIDS.

Elements. The smallest and most distinct variables that need to be considered in any situation. See S3 in the Table of Success Elements.

Environment. The full range of possibilities for success. See S1 in the Table of Success Elements.

Equivalent sets. In set theory nomenclature, this term represents an exclusive pairing of two elements from separate classes. In Theory *I*, this pairing aids in the creation of principles and the formation of strategies. The classes of Goals and Relationships form equivalent sets between their respective elements.

Exercises. The use of feedback and practice to fine-tune skills for success. See S4 in the Table of Success Elements.

Experiences. The first-hand knowledge gained from what an individual has observed, encountered, or undergone. See S2 in the Table of Success Elements.

Experiments. The tests, trials, or tentative procedures that an individual undertakes to apply a strategy for mapping potential to success. See S5 in the Table of Success Elements.

Failure. The result of important decisions made through ignorance or by default.

Fulfillment. The result of performance meeting or exceeding expectations based on potential. Using elements, principles, and strategies to align one's potential with one's performance assures success with fulfillment.

Full strategy. One element from each of the GRIDS classifications must be represented within this strategy. The full strategies will be used in the creation of a superstrategy.

Imagination. A source of unlimited ideas to explore that may result in success. See D4 in the Table of Success Elements.

Individuality. An individual's unique expression of will, found in self-directed efforts. See D5 in the Table of Success Elements.

Information. Accumulated, structured data that improves an individual's understanding of what is essential for the completion of a task. See D3 in the Table of Success Elements.

Instincts. Inborn characteristics which generate involuntary drives. *Instincts* help decide whether or not to expend energy in a given situation, depending upon the probability of a successful outcome. See D2 in the Table of Success Elements.

Instructions. Internal code (genes) and health condition that impacts the physical capability and mental alertness of an individual during performance. See D1 in the Table of Success Elements.

Interim strategy. A strategy that becomes necessary when a significant, critical problem is encountered while creating or executing a full strategy. Like a full strategy, an interim strategy encompasses key elements from each classification. The creation and execution of an interim strategy becomes necessary between exiting and resuming progress for the completion of a full strategy. Unlike a full strategy, an interim strategy is reserved for addressing the qualities or circumstances surrounding one person or one typically unanticipated event blocking progress.

Key element. An element that participates in the formulation of a strategy for a given situation. Each participant within a situation will likely require different key elements.

Management. The coordination of people and/or methods to enhance performances. See R1 in the Table of Success Elements.

Marketing. Discussions or suggestions that identify and attempt to satisfy the needs and wants of individuals. See R2 in the Table of Success Elements.

Mastery. The consistent development of expertise for increasing effectiveness. See R5 in the Table of Success Elements.

Matching. The bringing together of individuals' strengths and weaknesses to balance and complement each other for mutual benefit. See R3 in the Table of Success Elements.

Matrix. A structure that gives order to the elements and allows for their interaction. Each row offers a complete classification for consideration, and each column offers a perspective on interrelatedness. The five rows include Goals, Relationships, Ideologies, Determinants, and Steps. The acronym for these five areas is GRIDS.

Methodology. A system of methods founded upon elements and principles for use in scientific inquiry, analysis, and evaluation of given situations.

Ministry. The lending or receiving of support for self-assurance and direction. See R4 in the Table of Success Elements.

Opportunity/Challenge Survey (OCS). A tool for identifying problem areas and key elements that need to be addressed with strategies.

Overlapping sets. In set theory nomenclature, each successive element (from right to left in the Table of Success Elements) overshadows its predecessor. The elements in the Prime Determinants class represent overlapping sets.

Parallel strategies. 1. Strategies that support each other with a common direction. Parallel strategies do not permit sacrificing fulfillment of personal or corporate agendas. 2. Strategies that attack all significant barriers simultaneously (complete resolution within a relatively short period of time). This simultaneous consideration readily provides for strategic inclusion of every element affecting a given opportunity or challenge.

Principle. An accepted or professed rule of action built upon two or more elements that impact a particular situation.

Productivity. The abundance of an acceptable outcome.

Scientific methodology. A consistent approach for analyzing, understanding, and addressing situations. The order of steps for using a scientific methodology varies between scientists but includes the following: (1) Forming the hypothesis, (2) Observing and experimenting, (3) Interpreting the data, and (4) Drawing conclusion.

Set theory. The branch of mathematics that deals with relations between sets or arrangements of significant factors or elements. The detailed rules of operation and properties of the Table of Success Elements are best described through set theory. The rules of set theory establish relationships between each element in the Theory *I* Table of Success Elements.

Single-element strategy. A strategy built to address a key element.

Strategies. Step-by-step action plans that carefully consider all factors for attaining an objective or end result.

Subsets. In set theory, the occurrence of one element becoming subject to or under the influence of one other element within the same classification. The elements of the five Principal Ideologies are described in set theory nomenclature as subsets.

Superstrategy. An ordering of full strategies for the attainment of an end result. (Please see copyright page for the trademark description of this term.)

Symptom. Surface-level evidence of a problem without defining what it contains.

Table of Success Elements (TSE). This table contains five rows (classes) and five columns of elements pertaining to the creation of success from three points of view: (1) the "self" or person involved, (2) the "situation" or setting in which a person finds himself, and (3) the "strategy" that is the action plan for doing something about both the "self" and the "situation."

Theory *I*. This is a communication style that assumes results will be produced by providing a working environment where an individual is fulfilled while developing expertise to satisfy personal and corporate objectives. See I5 in the Table of Success Elements. Theory *I* is also a methodology supported by elements, principles, and strategies for ensuring success. (Please see copyright page for the registered trademark description of this term.)

Theory *I* axiom. A principle that has been developed, tested, and proven through the Theory *I* methodology.

Theory *M.* This is a communication style that assumes results will be produced by disrupting the entrenched habits of individuals to the point where they will strive to direct themselves toward greater effectiveness. See I4 in the Table of Success Elements.

Theory *X.* This is a communication style that assumes results will be produced by telling people specifically how to do what must be done. See I1 in the Table of Success Elements.

Theory *Y.* This is a communication style that assumes results will be produced by giving people the freedom to do what is most meaningful and gratifying to them. See I2 in the Table of Success Elements.

Theory *Z.* This is a communication style that assumes results will be produced by encouraging people to work cooperatively to support one another as a team. See I3 in the Table of Success Elements.

Universal sets. It is possible for any element in this class of elements to apply anywhere at any time in conjunction with any of the other elements. The elements of the five Fundamental Steps are described in set theory nomenclature as universal sets. When the members in this all-encompassing class of elements are joined with the other remaining elements in the Theory *I* Table of Success Elements, it is referred to as a universe.

Selected Bibliography

Cohen, Allan A., and David L. Bradford. *Influence Without Authority*. New York: John Wiley & Sons, 1990.

Gellerman, Saul W. *Motivation and Productivity*. New York: Amacom, American Management Association, 1963.

Goliszek, Andrew G. *Breaking the Stress Habit*. Winston-Salem: Carolina Press, 1987.

Gordon, Judith A. *Organizational Behavior*. 5th ed. Upper Saddle River: Prentice-Hall, 1996.

Graff, Harvey. *The World Book Encyclopedia*. 1997 ed., s.v. "Literacy."

Longenecker, Justin, Carlos Moore, and J. William Petty. *Small Business Management*. 10th ed. Cincinnati: South-Western Publishing Company, 1997.

McGregor, Douglas D. *The Human Side of Enterprise*. 25th Anniversary Printing ed. New York: McGraw-Hill, 1985.

McInerney, Francis, and Sean White. *The Total Quality Corporation*. New York: Truman Talley Books, 1995.

Myers, David G. *Psychology*. 4th ed. New York: Worth Publishers, 1995.

Peters, Thomas J., and Robert H. Waterman Jr. *In Search of Excellence*. New York: Harper & Row, 1982.

Restak, Richard, M.D. *The Brain*. New York: Bantam Books, 1984.

Vecchio, Robert P. *Organizational Behavior*. 3d ed. Fort Worth: The Dryden Press, Harcourt Brace College Publishers, 1995.

INDEX